ADVANCE PRAISE

In the extremely volatile and competitive nature of business environments across the globe today, values are an imperative for business success and sustenance. *Good Values, Great Business* presents a refreshing perspective to deal with this subtle subject of values in the context of business organizations. The pragmatic approach adopted by the authors makes the book a must-read for all business leaders, and those who are aspiring to be. I found the book very insightful and easily relatable.

Dr Pramath Raj Sinha, *Co-founder and Managing Director, 9.9 Media and Co-founder, Ashoka University*

I have often wondered if the core for building a lasting business is the values in it, why books on that have not been written. The reason could be that the founders of business who have been there for long did create a value system for their organization which was based on their personal value system and no one believed that any guidance is required for that—it is in you or not there.

At a time when start-ups are mushrooming and no one knows which ones would be unicorns or more, this is a fitting book that guides how to create a lasting one that maximizes returns on minimum strain in the entire system.

It takes through the entire life cycle of what 'value' is, establishing a case for its relevance and importance, its utility in business and on how to institute and nurture one. It is not an academic work but draws lessons from the various organizations and the experiences of people in them.

There is a common belief that wealth and values don't go together, and since business is meant to create wealth it cannot be value-driven. This book amply sets this to rest. Further, one may add the quote from *On Human Nature* by Arthur Schopenhauer, 'Who so lies quietly in his own will, like a child in the womb, and lets himself be led and guided by that inner principle from which he is sprung, is the noblest and richest on earth' (*Epistles*, 37).

It is a valiant attempt, and I hope there should be a series of such books so that Values occupy the centre stage in the organizational journey.

P. Venkatesh, *Director, Platforms and Solutions, Maveric Systems*

Wow ... I just kept going page after page with excitement and anticipation of what more would unfold in the book. The authors' basic belief in the subject of values and their core intent of helping others comes through as they articulate the concepts and also provide some structured mechanism for introspection and development of a value system for oneself. As very accurately stated in the notes, this book is a facilitator for anyone who wishes to seriously reinforce a culture of values in the organization.

S. Viswanathan, *Chief People Officer, NIIT Technologies Ltd*

Probably never before, the relevance of values and ethics in our life was more poignant and prominent than now and it is in this background that the advent of the book *Good Values, Great Business* by Br. Prasanna Swaroopa and T. D. Chandrasekhar, who have been the real practitioners of values and morals in their public lives, assumes so much significance and import.

This endlessly engrossing and thought-stimulating book, which I am very sanguine about, will not have only a limited range of readers, rather the book is for everyone. The open and honest examination of the issues concerning values and ethics which confront us daily in our life, be it within family or society, or at workplace, or within a team or in an organization or in an educational institution which will shape the destiny of the future India, etc., leaves an indelible imprint on the minds of readers, who in turn are enabled or handheld to tread a path of well-being and virtuosity. The unique experiment through use of 'Values Dialogues' in the book is really a trendsetter. It adds to the life and vitality of the book.

Last but not least, the kind of reflexivity and experiential learning which the reader gains through this book in the quest to achieve productivity, excellence, creativity, innovation and stress-free life adds to the seminal contribution made by the writers in their maiden endeavour.

S. K. Sinha, *Director (HR), Security Printing and Minting Corporation of India Limited*

Although there is a vast literature which educates us to make better business decisions, there is hardly any book which guides us to discriminate between what is wrong or what is right in business-related decision-making. The present book bridges this gap and reinforces that values in business are not a mere legal requirement, rather a foundation for sustainable and successful business leading to prosperity and welfare. The practice of values expounded in the book will lead one to achieve complete harmony in thoughts, actions and deeds in carrying out business activities.

P. V. Madhusudhan Rao, *Mehra Chair Professor, Department of Mechanical Engineering, IIT Delhi; Head, Department of Design, IIT Delhi*

In their lucid book *Good Values, Great Business*, Br. Prasanna Swaroopa and T. D. Chandrasekhar offer us a rational and vivid guide map of a very important region of our personal and professional lives, namely the topography and the terrain that are associated with values, dharma, guiding principles, ideals, morals, character, ethics, integrity and personal conduct. The book is written in a way that doesn't preach us. Instead, it offers us the prospect of evolving our own awareness of the large field upon which we traverse, and how values play an integral part in making our life's journey worthwhile and meaningful.

This highly readable book significantly elevates our understanding of values and draws out the deep connection between the creation of values and the significance of right values. An inspiring read, this book should be an essential reading for every person committed to creating a better, more equitable and just world.

Bharat Wakhlu, *Founder and President, The Wakhlu Advisory*

Values work like a glue which has the power to bind societies and organizations together in their quest to achieve common objectives. Values are not just some nice-to-have, feel-good corporate spiritualism but actually a business imperative which imparts long-term sustainability to organizational success, both in terms of business results and for ensuring a motivated and fulfilling people culture. And, in my experience, this is true across cultures and countries.

In this well-researched and well-articulated book, the authors explain this concept in a very simple and compelling way, making it a must-read for all those who want to develop strong organizations and personally develop as true leaders.

Mayank Trivedi, *President and CEO, Nestle Xiamen Yinlu Foods Company, People's Republic of China*

When a spiritual seeker and a business practitioner come together, they create magic! Having already read umpteen literature on values, still when I read this book, I found it very refreshing. It's contemporary, relevant, practical and timely. It reminds us what we already know—that values are core of any successful and sustained business—and then guides us where we often flounder—how to implement our value system in real life.

Shalabh Srivastava, *Country Director, RTI International India*

One can point to strong values or the lack of it behind the success or failure of every leader and business. Unfortunately, the quality of coverage of this important subject is still inadequate. Prasanna and TD have fulfilled a critical need of students and industry practitioners by providing a comprehensive, practical and easy-to-read book. *Good Values, Great Business* dispels the myth that strong values are primarily for fraud prevention. It lucidly explains how good values drive sustainable strong business performance. I hope that you would enjoy reading it as much as I did.

Sudip Mall, *President Director, Campbell Arnott's Indonesia*

GOOD VALUES, **GREAT** BUSINESS

GOOD
VALUES,
GREAT
BUSINESS

Br. PRASANNA SWAROOPA
T. D. CHANDRASEKHAR

Los Angeles | London | New Delhi
Singapore | Washington DC | Melbourne

First published in 2019 by

SAGE Publications India Pvt Ltd
B1/I-1 Mohan Cooperative Industrial Area
Mathura Road, New Delhi 110 044, India
www.sagepub.in

SAGE Publications Inc
2455 Teller Road
Thousand Oaks, California 91320, USA

SAGE Publications Ltd
1 Oliver's Yard, 55 City Road
London EC1Y 1SP, United Kingdom

SAGE Publications Asia-Pacific Pte Ltd
18 Cross Street #10-10/11/12
China Square Central
Singapore 048423

Published by Vivek Mehra for SAGE Publications India Pvt Ltd. Typeset in 10.5/13.5 pts Sabon and 9.5/14 pts ITC Stone Serif by Fidus Design Pvt. Ltd, Chandigarh.

Library of Congress Cataloging-in-Publication Data
Names: Swaroopa, Br. Prasanna, author. | Chandrasekhar, T. D., author.
Title: Good values, great business / Br. Prasanna Swaroopa, Spiritual Seeker,
    T. D. Chandrasekhar, Corporate Coach.
Description: Thousand Oaks : SAGE, [2019] | Includes bibliographical references.
Identifiers: LCCN 2019011943 | ISBN 9789353284558 (print (pb)) |
    ISBN 9789353284565 (e pub 2.0) | ISBN 9789353284572 (web) |
    ISBN 9789353284565 (e pub 2.0)
Subjects: LCSH: Business ethics. | Success in business.
Classification: LCC HF5387 .S93 2019 | DDC 174/.4—dc23
LC record available at https://lccn.loc.gov/2019011943

ISBN: 978-93-532-8455-8 (PB)

SAGE Team: Neha Pal, Sambhavi Shah, Madhurima Thapa and Rajinder Kaur

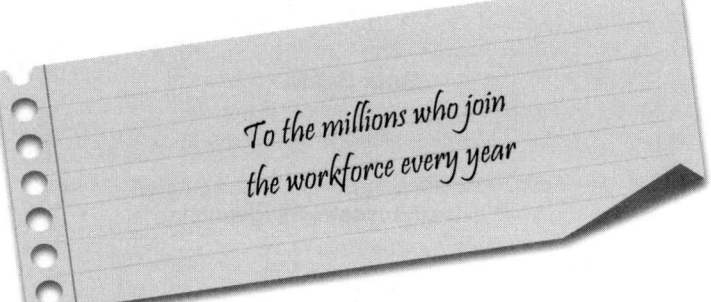

*To the millions who join
the workforce every year*

Thank you for choosing a SAGE product!
If you have any comment, observation or feedback,
I would like to personally hear from you.

Please write to me at **contactceo@sagepub.in**

Vivek Mehra, Managing Director and CEO, SAGE India.

CONTENTS

FOREWORD

Noted 20th-century poet, essayist, T. S. Eliot, said:

> Where is the wisdom we have lost in knowledge?
> Where is the knowledge we have lost in information?

To which, I as an economist will add, 'Where is the information lost in all the data?'

The Fourth Industrial Revolution dominated by the Internet, machine learning, social media and abundant data is changing careers and lives in profound and mundane ways. At the same time, never before has the planet been a home to so many people living longer lives and also moving vast distances, in real and virtual terms, in mind-boggling numbers. Also, humanity is faced with an enormous set of challenges as far as the natural environment is concerned. These set of cooperative and competing interactions among men, machines and Mother Nature will shape lives in ways that we have just begun to comprehend. While the media is full of stories about stresses and challenges in these relationships, we should also keep an eye on the many opportunities that will arise with a more positive impact.

How we cope in this world awash with data and information, and navigate our interactions with other people, as a student in a school or university, as a common citizen, or as an employee in an organization is very important and worthy of serious introspection.

It is against this backdrop that I laud the excellent attempt, *Good Values, Great Business* by Br. Prasanna Swaroopa and T. D. Chandrasekhar. The book is replete with appropriate and relevant case studies, anecdotes and interesting suggestions. But most importantly, it provides the framework and appropriate focus on 'values' and the critical role they play in how a business organization ought to conduct its internal affairs (with its employees) and external engagement (with clients, customers and partners) in this highly complex, interconnected, dynamic and diverse world.

The authors take a non-judgemental approach to the importance of values in today's business. Time spent by senior managers on thinking about and actively promoting values-based interactions and operations within their organizations is not to be seen as a waste of time or some checkbox requirement. It should become part and parcel of every business organization, no matter what stage of development it finds itself in.

I encourage the readers to read the book carefully and thoroughly, and constantly evaluate and re-evaluate their own morals and values orientation. It will be a time well-spent. But perhaps the biggest gift (to oneself and to your organization) is to take those principles, precepts and injunctions that are relevant and appropriate and internalize them—to commit yourself to a pursuit of good values to create a great business environment.

Dr Sunder Ramaswamy
Vice Chancellor
KREA University, Sri City, Andhra Pradesh

PREFACE

There is a lot of scepticism about the role of values in business. Values are merely seen as means to prevent fraud in accounting, billing, taxation, etc. In the context of a business organization, values are looked upon with apprehension, and at best are seen as an icing on the cake.

Somehow these prevalent views triggered a thought process in us, and sometime in early 2015, we felt the urge to address the topic of values.

We were fortunate to have had work environments, early in our careers, that were founded on values. To add to that, we were surrounded by individuals who were deeply committed to values and practised them. Because of these experiences, we were of the conviction that values are the very foundation of an organization—business or otherwise. The years of working in various organizations, and also outside, led us to believe that every team will fulfil its existence only when the members of the team espouse values.

Thus was born the idea of capturing our conviction and experiences in the form of a book, which can serve as a possible exposure to individuals and businesses, so as to reinforce the practice of values in business organizations and extending the same into all walks of life in our society.

During the course of our study and discussions with individuals across different kinds of industries, we felt that while there is respect for the idea of values, the same is not seen as a practical thing when it comes to business.

The founders and senior management of every organization need to explore this subject for wider application, so that they can build a strong organizational culture grounded on values, whereby the organization will be prepared to face any challenges and, needless to say, achieve business success. Above all, values are the only means to achieve sustainability of any business organization.

This understanding has to be realized by the founders and senior management, and instilled, nurtured and sustained in the very DNA of the organization for its success, innovation and long-term sustainability.

This book aims to guide anyone who wishes to understand the importance of values in the context of a business. Also, it acts as a facilitator to the senior management team, providing necessary inputs regarding the process of instilling values in organization. It proposes to eliminate the myths surrounding values, particularly in the context of business. Above all, the presentation aims to establish how values are the foundation to excellence, productivity, creativity and importantly creating a stress-free environment in the organization.

While this book directly addresses the issue of values in organizations, it is also an important companion for individuals. It captures experiences, challenges, inspirations and conflicts of individuals, and we believe the presentation will help individuals learn from these to fortify their own conviction regarding the importance of values.

This book was born of our deep-felt need to address this subject as an imperative for any organization, and not just as a nice-to-have and a nice-to-talk-about initiative in the organization and for its brochure.

Needless to say, this is a very vast subject, and it also means different things to different people. As you read on, you may feel that this book does not address such and such issues that are very important. Through this book, our intent is to give you a peep into this vast ocean, which the human civilization has tried to address generation after generation.

As you explore the subject along with us, you may find that you have different ideas and experiences through the years, and we fully respect that. While it has been our endeavour to bring a universal perspective, the subject of values will continue to challenge us because it is very perceiver dependent. In other words, how each one of us views a particular interaction or transaction will depend on our lens or perception.

Being aware of this challenge in front of us, our sincere intent and effort has been to make you aware of some of the different angles and perspectives. We hope this book will provide you with fresh perspectives and many new angles, and also force you to explore this very important subject of values in your context, in a manner beneficial to the ongoing values journey of your organization.

Let us strive together to build values-based organizations and thus values-based societies.

ACKNOWLEDGEMENTS

We, as authors of this book, sometimes wonder what led us to take up the subject of values as the focus of this book. When we dig deep, it is no wonder that both of us deeply felt a compelling need to address the subject of values. And the main cause of that is our respective families. It is the upbringing and the family setting that gave us the foundation of values that has sustained us throughout the years—through the different stages of our lives.

And for that we would like to begin by offering our gratitude to our parents and other members of our family, who, through their lives, have shown us the importance of values. Without their constant visible and invisible presence, even the idea of the book would not have been born.

We would like to express our deep sense of gratitude to Poojya Swami Bhoomananda Tirtha, who has been disseminating the spiritual wisdom of our land, showing the path to peace and happiness.

We also feel deeply indebted to the society and nation we are a part of, and particularly the culture we belong to. We also feel a deep sense of gratitude to our nation's great heritage, which undoubtedly has shaped our values.

We are extremely fortunate in having worked with colleagues who supported us through our corporate journey and reinforced our beliefs in values, particularly in the formative years of our professional careers. Many of them through their presence and actions demonstrated and guided us in this journey of values. To all those colleagues, we would like to express our deepest gratitude.

We have been very fortunate to have great friends who have been there in and through all phases and challenges of our lives. These friends have always shown us the mirror which has helped us grow. We know these friends will continue to share their love and warmth in the years to come also. To these special friends, we express our love and gratitude.

It is our deep conviction that the ideas of values are universal in nature. While languages, customs, traditions and belief systems may differ from country to country, the idea of values is universal. Values are the most universal and fundamental vocabulary of the humans on this planet. Because of this universality, great thinkers, including scientists, poets, novelists and philosophers, across generations, have continued to shape our thinking and inspired us in our lives. We would like to acknowledge and express our gratitude to all those great thinkers, who through their immortal words continue to guide us.

We would also like to thank SAGE for having taken up this manuscript for publication. In particular, we would like to express our gratitude to Manisha Mathews and her team, including Neha Pal and Sambhavi Shah, without whose constant support and insightful suggestions this book would not have reached culmination.

NOTES TO THE READERS

While the subject of values at one level seems very abstract, subjective and intuitive, at the same time it is also practicable, functional, pragmatic and rational. Above all, in the context of business organizations, it is realistic and beneficial.

At some instances in the book, we have mentioned some organizations along with their values. These have been taken from the website of the respective organizations (during the year 2018).

What this book is:

- It contains discussions on the various dimensions of the idea of values in the context of the functioning of any business organization.
- It discusses the fundamentals of the idea of values in the context of business, which enables the reader to adapt it to their organizational needs.
- It provides necessary guidelines to different stakeholders in the organization for creating an environment for meeting the business objectives.
- It acts as a facilitator to anyone who wishes to reinforce a culture of values in his/her organization.
- It makes the reader think and arrive at what is best for the situation, as this is not a subject where something can be prescribed.
- As such a subject cannot be dealt with in a linear or a step-by-step manner, it may appear to be repetitive at times, which is primarily because the reader is exposed to multiple perspectives.
- The attempt of the book is to allow the reader to evolve his/her own fundamental understanding of the subject of values, so as to enable him/her to carve out an appropriate path for his/her own organization.

- In a subtle subject like that of values, it is not always possible to make generic statements about values, because these are very personal to the culture of the organization. Therefore, this book poses questions at certain places, so that it makes you think about the topic at hand in the context of your organization and arrive at your answers or conclusions.

What this book is not:

- It is not a user manual or a process guide for implementation of a values-based culture in an organization.
- It is not a set of do's and don'ts regarding values, because the implementation depends on your organizational culture.
- It does not suggest right values, as the choices of values depend on your organizational needs and culture.
- It is not a textbook, presenting the subject from an academic perspective.

Points to Remember:

- The subject of values may appear to be very simple and too obvious because they are. But instilling and living the values is where the challenges present themselves. It calls for conviction and perseverance.
- What are critical values in one context (whether it is individual, family or organization) may not be as important in the another.
- Values are to be espoused; they need to become a part of the DNA of the organization.
- Do not adopt values, processes, guidelines etc. just because they sound nice and work well in another organization.
- This book does not adopt a case studies-driven approach. Thoroughly examine the needs of your organization and adopt what makes sense in your context.
- The examples discussed in this book, which are relevant to another organization and its context, may or may not directly apply in your context.
- On some occasions, the same idea would be presented in different contexts, from the point of view of different

stakeholders in the organization. This may seem as a repetition; it is not.

Values Reflection

We believe that asking the right questions and attempting to address them in the context of your organization will provide necessary insights that will be more relevant when it comes to discussing the values-based culture.

In general, books include a set of points summarizing the contents at the end of each chapter. In this book, we have presented a set of points or questions to introspect over, under the title 'Values Reflection' at the end of each chapter.

Introspect over the points presented repeatedly, so that you discover the relevance of these ideas in your context.

* * *

सुखार्थं सर्वभूतानां मताः सर्वाः प्रवृत्तयः ।
सुखं नास्ति विना धर्मं तस्मात् धर्मपरो भव ॥

All actions of all beings are for the sake of well-being, and without dharma (values-oriented living) there is no well-being. Therefore, follow the path of dharma.

—Subhaashitam

INTRODUCTION

Values Are Real

The stage was the Rostov Arena Stadium in Russia; the game was the knockout stage football (soccer) match between Belgium and Japan; the championship was the FIFA World Cup and the date was 2 July 2018.

Early in the second half (in the 48th and 52nd minutes), Japan had taken a lead with two goals to nil. With this lead, Japan's place in the quarter finals seemed certain.

But then, in the 69th and 74th minutes, came two goals from Belgium, levelling the match at two goals each. Soon the match had crossed the allotted 90 minutes of the game and moved into stoppage time.

While everyone thought the game would go into extra time, in the 94th minute came the winning goal from Belgium. The game was over! Belgium had won the game over Japan, three goals to two.

While the Belgian team and fans rejoiced, the Japanese team and supporters were in a state of consternation and shock. There were scenes of Japanese supporters breaking down in utter disbelief.

This was the scene just at the end of the game in the Rostov Arena Stadium!

What followed then was something that touched the entire football playing world. Setting aside what they had experienced—a heart-wrenching defeat—and that too after being so close to winning the game, the Japanese supporters were seen cleaning the stadium of trash left by the spectators in the stadium. What a wonderful gesture!

Also, what came to light later was that the Japanese team had left their changing room spotlessly clean along with a note that said 'spasibo' (Thank you in Russian). What a moving expression!

The Japanese football team had lost the game that day, but they had set a beautiful example for the entire world to follow!

Let us move from football to the world of business. There is lot of talk of 'values' in the world today. The business world too is buzzing with this word—values. Still a majority see the idea of values as something utopian, unpractical and far from reality. This non-believing population is convinced that it is not possible to have a culture of values, not only in a business organization but also in the society.

Let us examine this against the backdrop of what transpired that day in the football stadium. The following questions come to the mind of every individual, even those who are remotely thinking of the subject of values:

- What prompted the Japanese fans to collect trash from the stadium, when there is no expectation from the stadium administration?
- How did the Japanese fans imbibe this culture?
- Why did the Japanese fans engage in the act of cleaning, just after such a devastating loss? Let us not forget that the fans were gathered there with the sole aim of seeing their team win.
- What is the mindset of the Japanese football team that prompted them to act in such a graceful manner, even though they had just lost a crucial match, after being so close to tasting victory? Remember, with that loss, the Japanese team was knocked out of the tournament.
- What made the Japanese team and their fans to indulge in such an action, even though no one in the world would have questioned them, even if they had littered the place, after losing that game?

- Also, the Japanese football team and fans were guests in another nation. How did they retain their values of cleanliness even though they were in a foreign land?
- It is not just about a small group or a team. How did the entire Japanese people imbibe this value of cleanliness?
- How many years did it take for the Japanese culture to inculcate this quality of cleanliness?
- Knowing that to imbibe a quality like 'cleanliness' it will take many decades, and probably more than one or two lifetimes, why didn't the Japanese people say, 'let us not get into it'?
- Remember, Japan, as a nation, is faced with numerous natural catastrophes from time to time, and has also faced the aftermath of the atomic bomb. How is it that in spite of all that, as a culture, they have been able to imbibe this virtue of cleanliness?

The questions just do not seem to end. If we deeply introspect over these questions, we will definitely find answers to almost all these questions and doubts regarding the implementation of values in the context of a business organization.

When the entire Japanese population could imbibe this value of cleanliness, why should there be any doubt regarding imbibing it in an organization of a few 100 or 1,000 or 100,000 employees?

* * *

गुणैरुत्तमतां याति नोच्चैरासनसंस्थिताः।
प्रासादशिखरस्थोऽपि काकः किं गरुडायते॥

One achieves excellence and greatness because of one's values, not because of a high position. Just because it is perched at the top of a lofty palatial mansion, will a crow become an eagle?

—Chanakya Neeti

THE POWER OF VALUES

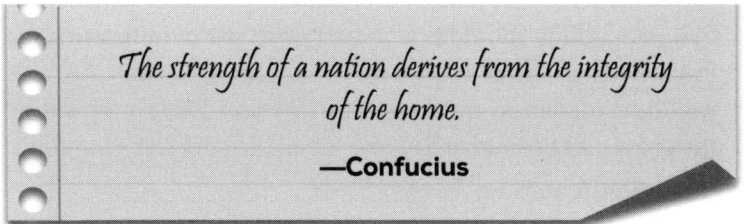

The strength of a nation derives from the integrity of the home.

—Confucius

'Honesty doesn't pay'.

'Values and business don't go together'.

'When there is a choice between values and profits, people always go for the latter'.

Whenever we casually mentioned the word 'values' to anyone, these were a few of the common reactions.

Note that these were instantaneous responses at the casual mention of the term values. It was as if most people intuitively knew that the idea of values in business is not something that made any sense. It was as if it was a no-brainer.

But whenever we sought a response on the subject over a serious discussion, with time in hand, the response was something entirely different.

Why this contrast in the response patterns? The 'why' is not the subject matter of this book. But it definitely prompted us to explore this subject in great detail. This exploration propelled us on an exciting journey regarding the subject of values in business.

Let us begin by using the oldest of approaches—narrating an old tale.

Once upon a time, there was a small kingdom in the east of India. Peace had reigned for many years there, ruled by a very able king. Following severe shortage of rains one season, the crops failed. Many people were hit by shortage of food supplies. The benevolent king announced various schemes to combat the situation. He had a tank placed in the middle of a district where citizens were relatively well-off. He had it announced that each family should bring just a small pot of milk and pour into the tank. And at the end of the day, the milk from the tank would be moved to the needy districts and freely supplied to the people. At the end of day one, when the tank was examined, it was found to be full of pure water.

What had happened?

Each one had thought: 'If I take and pour a pot of water and mix it in that tank of milk, nobody will notice the difference'. The only problem was everyone thought that way!

Let us transpose this situation into a business scenario. What are the possible ways to interpret the outcome?

- Each individual seems to think that even if there is a little dilution in values from my side, it is not going to change the overall outcome of the game.
- Upholding values is not my responsibility, it's somebody else's.
- Small violations will not adversely impact the business of society.
- I am generally a conscientious person, but these are difficult times.
- While the outcome was complete dilution (only water with no trace of milk), the strangely optimistic side to this thought process in people was 'everyone else is values-oriented'.

In our lives, we all might have experienced situations which are variations of this. I am also sure that in certain circumstances we can identify ourselves as the 'citizen carrying a pot of water to the tank'.

Businesses are similar to the foregoing situation. In all business endeavours, we have a number of individuals coming together to accomplish a task. Our values and thought processes eventually impact the final outcome of the business, whether we see it at the level of each activity, or as a series of projects over time.

Each individual has a role to play. Each individual matters. Each individual's thought process and values have an impact on the final result.

As is evident in the aforementioned social project of collecting milk for the needy, whenever one or more individuals participate together to achieve a particular task, values come into play and that undoubtedly impacts the final outcome.

Let's go beyond water and milk, into the real world of revenue and profits.

Values: The Thing That Makes It All Work

Let us examine one of the most frequent and important activities in any organization. At any time, it is going on somewhere or the other in the premises. Sometimes, it revolves around trivial issues, and at other times it involves extraordinary matters which can change the course of the entire organization. Yes, a 'meeting'.

There are all sorts of meetings held in each and every department. This is one place where the collective brainpower of individuals comes into play. Following is one anecdote, where the team is engaged in business planning:

The heads of the various departments have come together to finalize the business plan of the organization for the forthcoming year. The CEO begins by giving an overview of the past year and also sets the overall targets for the coming year. He reiterates the point that the targets are not negotiable. The Head of Sales and Marketing outlines the business plan, enumerating the targets for the different regions and product lines. She is unable to get any support from the Manufacturing department regarding the final dates of release of the new product. The Head of Personnel is unable to voice his concerns regarding the recently increased lead times in recruiting senior-level personnel. Head of Quality presents his plan and assures all his support for all quality checks.

Leaders of the organization need to ask themselves the following questions:

- Will this kind of an atmosphere yield the planned results of the organization?
- Will the prevailing environment help the organization to go beyond its capability and meet the demands of the fast-growing competition?
- Will this create inspired individuals who would find it exciting to stay with the organization?

Needless to say, this meeting will decide the fate of the organization and its functioning not only for the coming year but also for the years to come.

Can this meeting be successful, if the participants (this is just an indicative list):

- Do not 'trust' each other
- Do not 'support' each other
- Are not 'flexible' regarding their stance
- Do not 'respect' each other's views
- Do not have 'patience' to listen to each other
- Do not have 'integrity'
- Are not 'fair' in their demands
- Do not have 'empathy' towards others' constraints and limitations
- Do not 'accept' each other for what they are

If you examine any meeting (not just business planning meetings), you will find that some or many of these are exhibited. That is why meetings seldom produce the desired outcome.

On a closer look at the aforementioned list of qualities (the ones in quotes in the above list, such as trust, support, etc.), anyone will agree that whenever two or more individuals come together in order to work on anything, these qualities become essential for achieving the shared objective of the activity.

In the context of this book, these qualities or virtues are what we call values.

However strong the organization's systems, processes, procedures and guidelines are, underlying all of these are values. Can you imagine a system or process that succeeds in the absence of flexibility, integrity, trust, fairness? Seems rather impossible, doesn't it?

Let us not forget that an organization is a community of individuals and collaboration is at its core. It is not all about getting things done. Values come into play in every step of the way; it lends meaning and elegance to our actions even in the most trying circumstances. This is illustrated by what a senior manager with an information service provider shared with us.

> There was an employee I had to ask to resign—someone who had been a good project manager for almost nine years. However, in the beginning, he had submitted a false degree certificate and a recent reference check for all employees discovered this fact and for that he had to be let go. I was able to conduct the discussion in such a way that I upheld the dignity and respect for him as an individual. His capability as a project manager was separate from the violation of integrity committed by him to get into the organization. I told him that while he had violated a very core value of integrity by presenting false documents, he had been a good project manager. He left on a positive note and thanked our humane approach even while carrying out the tough decision of asking him to leave. Both respect for an individual and integrity are core values in our organization and it was tough to uphold both in such a scenario. I felt I was able to uphold both to my satisfaction.

Here, the Senior Manager has demonstrated that he could uphold values such as integrity, respect and compassion for a fellow employee in a very sensitive and trying situation.

Values Have a Context

The values that we are discussing in this book have a context. They are applicable in that context. And in that context, they have a specific interpretation.

Let us take the example of being open or transparent. This openness or transparency has to be interpreted as being transparent with each other in the context of the work involved. In the absence of the context, it seems like 'sharing everything I know'. And that seems rather threatening. Hence, people immediately step back or become defensive when it comes to adopting such a value.

Similar is the case with honesty. We are not saying 'be honest'. There is a difference between being honest and being honest with each other in the context of the work involved at the workplace.

Whenever we talk about honesty, that honesty has a context. If you just say, 'I am truthful', the universe of that is too large. It is vague and intimidating. But if you say, 'I will be truthful to you, in our interactions, in our relationship at the workplace, in the scope of the work involved', then the boundaries are clear and defined.

So in the case of the team also, 'I shall be honest to the team' means that if there is a problem at work, I shall be honest and share it with the team.

We are saying, 'if there is a problem, that relates to us, as members of a team', we are not referring to 'my personal problems at home or elsewhere'.

As far as we are concerned, as a team, let us make this a workplace where we find comfort and joy in working together and in keeping the interactions stress-free.

So, in a way, we are relaxing the constraints. Relaxing the constraints makes it feasible and then it provides us with a way to address the problem. Otherwise the problem seems and perhaps will be insurmountable.

Also, let's be realistic. 'I shall be honest' as a goal will take us a lifetime, but 'I will be honest to my team' at least gives you a handle to begin with.

Productivity, Excellence, Innovation

We began the discussion on values in the background of meetings held in the organization. If values are so relevant in the context of meetings, what would be the importance of these values in the case of organizations which rely on innovation and creativity to stay in business? Organizations like Google and Pixar increasingly talk of 'bringing together people from diverse backgrounds, who are energetic, passionate individuals, and have unconventional approaches to work, play, and life'.

Such collaboration and synthesis will not be possible in the absence of these values!

According to a study by the Center for Creative Leadership, empathy is positively related to job performance. The study goes on to assert that empathy is a construct that is fundamental to leadership.

A critical foundation of any organization is teamwork. Individually, team members may be great performers, but if the appropriate values are missing, they fail to come together as a team and a single cohesive unit. Not only are they ineffective as a team, they also fail to bring out their best. On the contrary, even if they are not individually great performers but there is a presence of certain values (such as flexibility, empathy, respect for others, integrity, patience, etc.), they can become very effective as a team, because of effective synthesis of diverse capabilities.

Going Beyond Systems, Processes, And So On

It is time we introduce the key term that is the core theme of this book—values. Like many other very important things in life, values are hard to define!

Following are some examples of values: humility, compassion, honesty, integrity, trust, empathy, patience, tolerance, acceptance, flexibility and altruism.

When we refer to the term values, it has been observed that there is a general common understanding of what it means. You may not get a common crisp definition of values, but everyone knows what you are talking about. When you refer to the term 'values decline', nobody has a doubt about what you are talking about.

For the purpose of this book, we define values as:

> Any quality or principle relating to the human personality with regard to the individual's attitude and/or conduct, as a means or as an end in itself, which makes the interaction between one or more individuals pleasant, effective, productive and harmonious, in the context of workplace, family, society or nation.

We are deliberately defining the term in its plural form.

Seeing the aforementioned examples, one may say these are virtues. When you reflect on why we are discussing values, you will appreciate that the terms values and virtues are very similar.

Outlining his philosophy on corporate management, Ray Dalio (founder of the investment firm Bridgewater Associates), in a publication called *Principles* says, 'values are what you consider important, literally what you "value". Principles are what allow you to live a life consistent with those values. Principles connect your values to your actions; they are beacons that guide your actions'.

Values provide meaning and purpose to all human actions. There are various terms that you may come across—human values, organizational values, universal values, eternal values, etc. If you examine all of these closely, they are one and the same. Yes, of course, we are talking of human values. For the purpose of this presentation, it is not very important to get into these individual terms.

By bringing in arguments that values will differ over time (contemporary values), society (societal values), region (regional values), etc., we will be deviating from the very purpose of values. Particularly, in today's context of globalization, values are the universal vocabulary. For two employees—one who comes from Southeast Asia and another who comes from Europe—the language of one may be alien to another, but the vocabulary of values—kindness, empathy, camaraderie, trust, integrity, compassion—are universal.

Although values may be integrated in and through the systems and processes that we have, they transcend processes too. That is what makes values alive and relevant to the context of workplace interactions. This is illustrated by what we heard from a young executive who worked at the head office of an IT company.

> Early in my career, on one windy winter night, I had worked late in office and was leaving for home. I was entitled then to take a ride back home by an auto-rickshaw and have the fare reimbursed. The auto-rickshaw ride in a wintry night wouldn't have been a pleasant experience. I was waiting outside the office gate. A senior executive passing by stopped at the gate and asked me to take a taxi and said that he would sign for the same. This care for a fellow employee made the workplace a very homely place—known both for excellence at work and the joy it gave working there.

This demonstration of care and concern went beyond standard procedures adopted by the organization. There are many situations where we have to interpret the processes and procedures to make them relevant to the context we are in.

Organizational Culture

Let us explore the term organizational culture, which everyone is familiar with. Every organization has a culture that everyone identifies with, whether it is formally stated or otherwise. Let us examine the definition given by David Needle: 'organizational culture represents the collective values, beliefs and principles of organizational members'. He goes on to add: 'culture includes the organization's vision, values, norms, systems, symbols, language, assumptions, environment, location, beliefs and habits'. According to the *Business Dictionary*, 'organizational culture encompasses values and behaviours that contribute to the unique social and psychological environment of an organization'.

When employees of an organization say, 'this is how we do things here; this is what we are', they are actually giving an idea of their organization's culture.

If we now break down the organization's culture into its constituents, we ultimately find that the most basic building blocks are nothing but values.

Values are not about having some nice sounding statements as a part of the organization's vision and corporate communications. They are the very foundation of the organization's business success and culture. Values are what deliver productivity, innovation and excellence. Merely seeing values as just adhering to some rules would be missing the entire point.

All Organizations Already Have Values in Place

This is perhaps the most important thing anyone who is on the journey of instilling values in an organization has to realize—we already have values. In other words, no organization can say 'we are devoid of values'.

Let us hear what a senior consultant with one of the world's leading management consulting firms had to say:

Our firm is one of the premier management consulting firms. At that point of time, I was a fairly young management consultant wanting to work hard and add substantial value to the clients. One of the projects we had was on valuation. We were suggesting a financial option and my task was to do the financial analysis and send the initial recommendation to the client. Our firm prided itself on excellence at work. This particular work was important, as the calculations I was doing were pivotal in coming to a particular decision. I put in a lot of effort and completed the work and sent it to the client and the working also supported the existing preferred outcome.

A day later, out of the blue, I realized a silly mistake I had made in an assumption. It was an error which had just slipped past me and this error made a big difference to the final output. The partner who was in charge of this particular assignment was known to be a stickler for attention and had a reputation to be a tough task master and my own experience supported that. I decided to meet him the first thing in the morning the very next day. Meanwhile, I had also emailed him about my mistake. I feel sheepish remembering it now, but I had my resignation letter with me. I was certain that as soon as I entered his room, I would have to bear the brunt of his anger and his tirade at letting the client down.

As soon as I entered the room feeling really anxious, the first thing I heard from him was: 'I know, you must be feeling upset. Let's sit down and review the work again and see what we now need to tell the client'.

I still remember the relief I felt and how grateful I felt towards my senior. I realized why he was so loved, in spite of being such a hard task master at work. Along with excellence, caring for people, especially when they needed it most, was clearly his strength and a value he demonstrated.

We would have had similar experiences during our years in different roles in different organizations. What do these situations demonstrate? In the aforementioned episode, we saw the demonstration of empathy, care, allowing mistakes, acceptance of the situation and forgiveness. And we may have come across such experiences, even in the absence of formal declaration of values in the organization.

This is why we say that every organization, irrespective of the size, industry, structure, etc., already has values which are holding the organization together.

If at all, all we need is to improve upon or fine-tune them.

So there is nothing called starting from scratch.

Values are not just icing on the cake, they are the cake!

Some consider the subject of values as something antagonistic to business. 'Let us focus on business, with values you can't run a business', they say.

Work in all business organizations is all about teamwork—individuals coming from varied backgrounds, different skill levels, divergent ideas and, most important of all, having diverse personalities. Collaboration amongst departments and individuals is the key to an organization's success. Effective collaboration among individuals is not possible unless at least some of these values are lived by the individuals: compassion, ability to learn from others, trust, flexibility, acceptance, empathy, forgiveness, camaraderie, patience, generosity, to name just a few. These qualities are imperative for achieving the goals of the teams.

An organization is all about teamwork, effective interaction and collaboration among individuals. Unless these and many other values, both at the individual and team level, are actively nurtured and facilitated, meeting and excelling the business goals will become an uphill task.

Bridgewater Associates ($150 billion hedge fund) records all its employees' conversations/meetings, taking transparency and openness to a completely different level. While in the initial stages, the employees found it very challenging, in the long run it has had tremendous benefits in furthering the business to new heights.

Values Dialogues

Daily at the workplace, we face a number of situations where our values are put to test. We face dilemmas, conflicts, questions, critical remarks, etc., and we have to deal with them in real time. These are part of business situations, some of which decide the course of the organization and the business you are in.

These situations are of numerous varieties and each situation is different from the other. We cannot possibly imagine and discuss the infinite possibilities of challenging situations.

However, here we present a series of conversations titled 'Values Dialogues' at the end of each chapter that provides a perspective to a possible line of thinking that through introspection will give you greater clarity in dealing with these situations of conflict. These may not provide you the absolute solution for the situation you have at your workplace, but they attempt to expose you to a possible line of thinking that might take you in the direction of a solution. It would be presumptuous on our part to attempt to provide answers to all those unique and complex situations each of us face at the workplace every day. This is more of a means to introspect than to provide concrete solutions.

These dialogues are presented as a series of questions and answers between Sheela, a senior vice-president and a mentor with a large MNC, and Sanjay, who has recently taken over as a team lead in the same organization.

Sanjay: We, in this organization, are talking of values all the time, and we stress on the point that good values will lead us to success in business. But in the morning when I open the newspaper and read about successful organizations, they are not particularly known for their values. In such a backdrop, where is then the inspiration or motivation for being values-oriented?

Sheela: You have addressed an important point, Sanjay. There are two parts to your question—successful organization and inspiration/motivation—and I would like to address the first. What is a successful organization in your opinion?

Sanjay: An organization which is doing very well financially in its own space, an organization that plays a pioneering role in the industry and one where the employees are taken care of.

Sheela: Are you sure those are the only parameters? We need to really examine this point. I agree that the organization has to perform well financially, and that's an important fuel for survival. There are a few other elements too that are very crucial—one relates to the employee and another relates to sustenance.

The organization has to keep the well-being and success of its own employees in mind. That means the employees should want to belong to the organization, wish to grow with the organization and wish to build a long-term relationship with the organization.

The other key aspect is that the organization is very consciously working towards its sustenance over a long period of time. Do you know what the average life span of a company is?

Sanjay: No clue. Never thought about it.

Sheela: The average life of business organizations across the world is becoming shorter; it is 12.5 years in Japan and Europe, and 18 in Germany.[1]

Sanjay: That's shocking.

Sheela: Yes. Isn't that a cause for concern? So organizations need to think about ways and means that will ensure their sustenance, and we know that values are the foundation for sustenance. Let us not forget, even civilizations failed to survive because of decay of values. So we don't have a choice in creation of a values-based culture. It is an imperative. It is the oxygen for our survival as an organization.

Sanjay: I understand that part. But how do we generate the inspiration or motivation to adopt them at an individual level?

Sheela: Each of us will have to think about that. The motivation is survival, else soon, we will not have an organization to be part of. The inspiration has to come from within us. That is what will sustain this movement towards creation of a

[1]*Source*: Stratix Group in Amsterdam.

Good Values, Great Business

values-based culture. People often ask, 'But what's in it for me?' What do you feel Sanjay?

Sanjay: I feel there is something more than survival here. The joy of work is also in doing things well, excellence, innovation, quality, etc. And I feel that all these are enabled by a culture that inspires these and provides an environment for enjoying the work we do. And that comes from values alone.

Sheela: You have made a wonderful point there, Sanjay. It is up to the organization to create that kind of environment, and each of us will have to play our part in that.

Values Reflection

Introspect and deliberate upon these questions, in the context of your organization, as you go forward in strengthening your organization's culture of values:

- What is your organization's focus and objective while considering the subject of values?
- In the name of values, are you just trying to ensure that as an organization you adhere to the laws of the land or is there something more?
- What are the values that will help your organization's growth parameters, such as revenue, profits, innovation, etc.?
- Is corruption just related to fraud in accounts, finance and intellectual property?
- List at least five points that define your organization's culture.

* * *

परोपकाराय फलन्ति वृक्षाः परोपकाराय वहन्ति नद्यः।
परोपकाराय दुहन्ति गावः परोपकारार्थमिदं शरीरम् ॥

Trees bear fruits for the welfare of others; rivers flow for the
welfare of others; cows give milk for the welfare of others; and
the human body is meant for the welfare of others.

—Subhaashitam

2 Chapter

CONFUSION OVER NOMENCLATURE

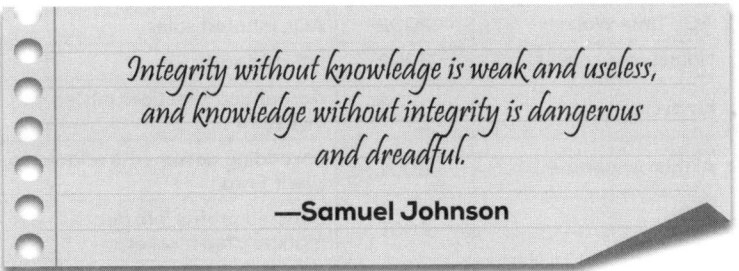

Integrity without knowledge is weak and useless, and knowledge without integrity is dangerous and dreadful.

—Samuel Johnson

Values Are Not Just about Preventing Fraud

For some years now, a lot has been written and spoken about the subject of integrity in business—more specifically accounting practices and fraud prevention.

When we discuss the subject of 'values' with anyone, the first impression they have is that it is something to do with addressing malpractices in the business. And that too typically revolving around accounts and finance matters. Since the subject often has drama and scandal associated with it, it attracts more attention.

Table 2.1 shows some of the financial fraud cases that drew worldwide attention.

Table 2.1 Some Worldwide Scams and Scandals		
Company	**Year**	**Allegations**
Punjab National Bank Scam	2011–2018	Fraudulent letter of undertaking worth crores
Commonwealth Games	2010	Spending was far less than what was declared
Satyam Computers	2009	Manipulating balance sheet

(Table 2.1 continued)

(Table 2.1 continued)

Company	Year	Allegations
Bernie Madoff Scandal	2008	Bernie Madoff was alleged in $50 billion fraud
Lehman Brothers	2008	Covered up billions in loans disguised as sales
Fannie Mae and Freddie Mac	2008	Earnings were misstated
AOL Time Warner	2002	AOL inflated sales
Homestore.com	2002	Inflated sales
Kmart	2002	Accounting practices misled investors
Arthur Andersen	2001	Shredding documents related to client Enron
Enron	2001	Boosted profits, hid debts; manipulated market
Xerox	2000	Falsifying financial results, boosting income

A study conducted by Assocham and Grant Thornton revealed that corporate frauds have increased by 45 per cent in the last two years.

Many studies have been conducted to analyse financial frauds and figure out steps to prevent or at least minimize them. Needless to say, when large amounts are involved, amounting to millions or even billions, the news attracts attention from everyone—concerned or not concerned.

Much has been written and talked about financial frauds. However, that is not the subject matter of this book. So when we talk of values, our attention is not on fraud prevention. But values will definitely address this problem as well in a very fundamental way.

Are Frauds Only Money-Related?

Fraud exists across different industries; no segment is safe from the extending clutches of corruption and fraud. Conventionally, we associate fraud with bribery, money laundering, tax evasion, asset misappropriation, accounting, etc. Fraud extends beyond these areas into payroll, piracy, intellectual property, manufacturing, marketing, etc. Following is a brief description of such cases:

- Marketing: Fraudulent practices for the promotion of a product or service. For example, false claims about product or service, or not fully disclosing limitations or side effects of products, very commonly seen by way of exaggerated presentations to customers.
- Personnel management: Dressing up resumes to project skills and capabilities which do not exist, and allocating inexperienced personnel to projects (as opposed to agreement with clients) are common occurrences.
- Product quality: Lower quality goods and services which are released knowing fully well that they do not meet the required specifications.
- Process quality: Organizations manipulate and fudge process records to show compliance and get ISO and other such certifications. This common violation goes beyond mere records and hits at the very root of product and process quality.
- Intellectual property: In segments where products are the backbone of business, adopting illegal means to gain knowledge of competitors' products and business plans. One of the most common violations is the use of software without appropriate licences.

It is clear that fraud extends beyond accounts and finance. In fact, it can exist in every function of an organization.

Values Are Not about Codes to Prevent Fraud

For many people, the mention of the word values in the context of a business organization brings to mind Code of Conduct to prevent instances of frauds in the workplace. Most people we have talked to think that having values in a practical sense is about preventing fraud, bribery, money laundering, tax evasion, asset misappropriation, fraudulent accounting, copyright and other IP violations, etc. While it is financial fraud that gets maximum attention, values are not just about preventing malpractices in finance and accounts.

In his study presented in the book *Good to Great*, Jim Collins refers to traits such as modesty, humility and fearlessness in the context of Level 5 leaders. What are these? Yes, they are values to be inculcated.

Most of the senior executives we surveyed emphatically say that values apply to all employees at all levels in the organization, although they believe that senior management should lead the way.

Zappos.com's (a major online retailer acquired by Amazon) core values include the following: be open-minded, build open and honest relationships with communication, build a positive team and family spirit, do more with less, be passionate and determined, be humble. Indian Oil Corporation has identified care (which includes empathy), innovation, passion and trust as its core values.

Here, we see how business organizations have identified humility, open relationships, open-mindedness, empathy, etc., as values that are critical to their business success.

A senior executive in a financial services organization shared the following episode, saying that he was exposed to a new dimension to fairness. He felt that the organization did something which was beyond the established practices.

I had resigned from a financial services corporation for my new role in another organization. My date of leaving was in February that year. Technically, our performance was appraised till December end and the bonus was decided based on the performance till then. It usually was decided by February end and disbursed a month later. I was pleasantly surprised to receive my bonus by cheque at home, after I had exited and had my full and final settlement. The head of the business unit I was a part of in the previous organization felt that I had performed well and deserved the bonus. He could have easily not taken that decision.

This experience told me that being fair matters even when you don't expect anything in return as in this instance there was nothing that person was going to get out of this decision except maybe a good feeling of having been fair and perhaps my goodwill!

How do you define this behaviour? This may not even figure in the Code of Conduct of the organization. However, such actions by individuals and organizations go a long way in establishing a relationship, which transcends the boundaries of the organizations.

Everyone Is Talking about Business Ethics

These days, we come across the phrase 'business ethics' quite often; we hear of workshops, conferences, seminars, papers, articles, etc., where business ethics is the theme. Organizations have policies, processes, training and audits that address the topic of ethics.

Here is a commonly accepted definition of business ethics: 'Business ethics are ethical principles and moral or ethical problems that arise in a business environment. It applies to all aspects of business conduct and is relevant to the conduct of individuals and entire organizations'.

What does the term ethics mean? Ethics, in simple terms, are principles and values that govern the behaviour and conduct of an individual or a group or a society. In that, it is very fundamental in nature and at the very fulcrum of human personality, guiding and giving effect to any behaviour or interaction with reference to (directly or indirectly) other individuals, society, nation and the entire globe.

Let us begin with the phrase itself—business ethics. What should it be? What are we aiming to achieve by introducing this subject of business ethics, ethics in business or ethics of business in the context of business?

Based on examining much of the discourse going on in this area, it appears that the corporate world is trying to focus its attention on the following:

- How to ensure that there is no corruption (with the specific interpretation as graft) in any of the dealings, in any of the functions of the business?
- How to ensure that departments such as accounting, sales, products, billing, etc., adhere to practices which are legal and are as per standards?

A few decades ago, when quality was the mantra across all industries, the term 'quality' was defined as conformance to requirements. In the context of ethics, are we trying to find a similar definition for ethics? In other words, what we are trying to achieve is to ensure that the organization in each of its functions is adhering to the law of the land.

Does that mean we don't need the subject of business ethics?

No, certainly not. We, as humans, need the necessary rules, procedures, processes and systems to ensure that we do not end up violating the laws of the land. Yes, policing is necessary, not only in the society but also in business organizations.

We came across this narrow definition of business ethics in *Investopedia*:

> Business ethics is the study of proper business policies and practices regarding potentially controversial issues, such as corporate governance, insider trading, bribery, discrimination, corporate social responsibility and fiduciary responsibilities. Law often guides business ethics, while other times business ethics provide a basic framework that businesses may choose to follow to gain public acceptance.

Most people perceive business ethics as addressing the right and wrong related to the conduct of the business. Functionally, it deals with the transactional issues (in the context of what is right and what is wrong) in finance, human resources, sales and marketing, production, property, intellectual property, etc.

Have we narrowed down the definition of ethics in the context of business too much? When this question is raised, the typical response from the proponents of business ethics is that we are not aiming at making people good, honest, kind, altruistic, etc. Agreed! That will be too broad a scope and also an ambitious one, if it is spoken of in general terms.

Can prevention of fraud, corruption and graft enhance the effectiveness of an organization and its employees? Can it help in achieving and surpassing its targets? Can it help in innovation and in taking the organization to its next level?

Going beyond the Limited Definition of Business Ethics

During one of the studies carried out, we interviewed a number of individuals from across different organizations, at different levels, to understand how they view values (we used this word as is, without defining it) in the context of their organizations. We came across the following episode:

> There is an organization in the Information Technology sector which is involved in providing technology-based products and services to clients across the world. There is a team which is engaged in developing a solution for a complex business situation, involving latest technology. In the course of the project, the team is faced with a very complex problem which is very crucial to the final solution. Sanjay, the designer and architect of the team, is one who can solve this problem. However, Sanjay has been unhappy at work over a period of time. Even though he can solve this problem, he is very uncooperative, though in very subtle ways. The net result being the team not being able to get over the hurdle effectively.

The following important points come to light:

- This is most probably not a direct violation of any of the business ethics as established by the organization.
- None of the prevalent policies, contracts, processes or audits will ever be able to address this violation.

Why Not Use Terms Like Ethics and Morals?

Is the idea of business ethics wrong? A simple and straightforward answer is 'no'. It however depends on how you have adopted the definition in your organization.

Here is what the dictionary (Dictionary.com) says regarding the word ethics: 'deals with values relating to human conduct, with respect to the rightness and wrongness of certain actions and to the goodness and badness of the motives and ends of such actions'.

Even the term moral is defined similarly—'founded on the fundamental principles of right conduct rather than on legalities, enactment or custom'.

During our surveys, we found that whenever we used terms like ethics or morals, employees found it very intimidating.

Why? The answer is quite simple. Whenever people confronted decisions relating to right or wrong, or good or bad, they found it threatening.

This is the reason why we chose the term values, as against ethics and morals. The idea will become clearer as we progress further with our discussions.

Then What Is Code of Conduct?

The International Federation of Accountants (in its 2007 International Good Practice Guidance) provided the following working definition for Code of Conduct: 'Principles, values, standards, or rules of behaviour that guide the decisions, procedures and systems of an organization in a way that (a) contributes to the welfare of its key stakeholders, and (b) respects the rights of all constituents affected by its operations'.

Many organizations use the term 'Code of Conduct' to include the following:

- Core values
- Qualifications of products or services

- Qualities that define how you approach work
- Commitment to adhere to the law of the land
- Commitment to society and environment

Code of Conduct Implemented as Do's–Don'ts

There are many organizations that have adopted some values or principles and named them Code of Conduct. The attempt of a Code of Conduct is to instil values and principles among the employees across the different departments and locations of the organization, thereby establishing and sustaining a culture of values.

Any employee, who joins the organization, is expected to go through this Code of Conduct and sign off his or her acceptance, and thereby commit to live by those codes.

However, the term code is defined as 'a systematically arranged collection or compendium of laws, rules or regulations' (according to WordReference.com). Perhaps because of this, some organizations have implemented their Code of Conduct as a list of rules individuals belonging to the organizations must adhere to.

In order to explore this subject further, let us examine the Code of Conduct of the upper house of the Parliament (Rajya Sabha) in India. Here are some of the points from the list[1]:

- Members must not do anything that brings disrepute to the Parliament and affects its credibility.
- Members must utilize their position as members of Parliament to advance the general well-being of the people.
- Members should not lend ready support to any cause of which they have no or little knowledge.
- Members should not misuse the facilities and amenities made available to them.
- Members are expected to maintain high standards of morality, dignity, decency and values in public life.

[1]For the complete list, visit http://rajyasabha.nic.in/rsnew/members/code_conduct.pdf

It is true that one cannot fundamentally argue with these points. They are essential or at least they have been considered essential by the organization which has adopted them.

Examining the aforementioned set of codes, following are some thoughts that come to mind:

- We should ensure that in adhering to a Code of Conduct, which has been presented as a checklist of do's and don'ts, we do not lose the intent and spirit behind ethics.
- Is it practically possible to make a complete and comprehensive list of do's and don'ts which addresses all possible opportunities of violations?
- Presented in this manner, does it inspire the members of the organization to adhere to them and above all contribute to excellence in the organization?
- This list is only addressing possible areas of transgressions. It is not in any way contributing to the productivity, efficiency, excellence, etc.

Which Terms Do Organizations Use?

Different organizations use different terms to capture their values, principles or whatever else you include in your commitment to values. Following are some examples:

- Core values: Cognizant, Zappos
- Code of Conduct: Google, Hershey's
- Code of Business Conduct: Coca-Cola
- Business Ethics and Compliance: Starbucks

Cognizant's core values:

- Transparency
- Passion
- Empowerment
- Collaboration
- Customer focus
- Integrity

Source: https://www.cognizant.com/about-cognizant/cultural-values (accessed on 9 April 2019)

PepsiCo's global Code of Conduct:

All PepsiCo employees are expected to embrace the principles of our code and:

- Show respect in the workplace.
- Act with integrity in the marketplace.
- Ensure ethics in our business activities.
- Perform work responsibly for our shareholders.

Source: https://www.pepsico.com/about/global-code-of-conduct (accessed on 9 April 2019)

Finally, here are the various terms that are in use:

- Core values
- Code of conduct
- Code of ethics
- Business ethics
- Principles
- Values

The choice of the term depends on the organization and the prevailing culture. There are organizations which use more than one of these terms. For example, Procter & Gamble uses both the terms values and principles in their 'Our Purpose, Values and Principles' document.

It is up to the management of the organization to adopt a term that aligns with the vision, mission and culture of the organization. What is more important is to examine whether the values chosen help the employees to focus on the shared purpose of the organization towards achieving the objectives of the organization.

When we mentioned the term values, many of the respondents during our study asked, 'Is that not what virtues are all about?' Some said, 'values are deeply held principles and beliefs'. While others felt that they prefer the term value system.

Well, broadly speaking, all these terms convey the same thing. We could have gone with any of these terms. Terms such as compassion, empathy and integrity are virtues. But the term virtue also implies or suggests goodness or righteousness. But what is important in the context of the business organization is what matters to the organization with regards to the business. In other words, 'What the organization values the most!' Thus, we prefer to use the term values.

Thus, we have chosen the term values as the focus of the book, because at a fundamental level that is what all these various terms address.

Remember, values are not just about preventing fraud, transgressions and infringements; they are about excellence, productivity, quality, innovation, creativity and so on.

Values Dialogues

Sanjay: In all its communications, the senior management is always talking about business goals in terms of revenue and growth. Because of this system of incentives for performance and the need to survive in the organization, the entire atmosphere has become extremely competitive. Where is the place for values in this highly intense and competitive workplace?

Sheela: You have described the context well. That indeed is the nature of many a workplace today. Let us discuss each of the aspects separately, and see where they lead us. First of all, the idea of business goals. This is the reason we are here. The importance of the business goal cannot be set aside. Then what in your opinion seems to be the problem?

Sanjay: It is this constant pounding of the idea of numbers, billing, revenue and profits. I do recognize the importance of it all. But is there not a better way of doing it? In this way the organization comes across as a ruthless one.

Sheela: I understand what you are saying. All organizations eventually have to meet their business goals. However, the style of management has a big role to play in how the intentions of the management are perceived. This is also a case for relevant values for the senior management of the organization to exhibit. Even though chasing numbers, the management team needs to be seen as caring, empathetic and fair in the eyes of the employees. And the only solution there is values. The senior management team needs to imbibe and demonstrate the following values—empathy, fairness, humility, integrity and transparency.

Sanjay: Aren't these critical values for managers at all levels?

Sheela: Absolutely, it is critical for managers at all levels to live these values. Only then, the work environment will be free from pressures of numbers.

Sanjay: Do the pressure of numbers actually go away?

Sheela: Not really, the pressure will always be there. But you don't feel the pressure. It then seems like a healthy challenging environment and you begin to enjoy the work. Similarly, the performance incentives and bonuses are part of the work culture today. Most organizations have the system of variable compensation that is driven by performance.

Sanjay: But since the environment is free from the pressure, these things do not disturb the employees.

Sheela: Exactly! Then you actually have individuals wanting to excel and it is not because of pressures, but because they want to do well. You end up creating a healthy competitive environment. You are not competing with each other, but, subconsciously, you are inspiring each other to perform better. Also, remember that creativity and innovation are possible only when the work culture is free from pressure, tension and stress. To conclude, the presence of values has created a culture where you are promoting excellence, creativity and quality, while at the same time, at the top of it all, the revenue and profit targets are automatically met.

Sanjay: In short, what you are saying is that the pressure of number targets is aggravated by what kind of signals senior management emits, and the same can be diffused merely by how the management team conducts itself, demonstrating values such as empathy, fairness, humility, integrity and transparency.

Sheela: You have summarized it well. However, it is an ongoing journey that calls for patience, perseverance, sincerity of intent and above all commitment to the cause of values. Also, it is not as easy as it sounds. It is a long journey and the management team has to be alert and sensitive to changing times and recalibrate itself from time to time to be able to sustain a culture which is free from pressures of any kind.

Values Reflection

Introspect and deliberate upon these questions, in the context of your organization, as you go forward in strengthening your organization's culture of values:

- Which term has your organization used to instil values in your organization and why?
- What are the various potential areas of transgressions in your area of business? What means do you see of preventing them?
- Examine the Code of Conduct of PepsiCo (listed earlier). What will be the relevance of these codes in the context of your organization?
- In the context of your organization and given your culture, what will be the impact of using a term like moral code in your organization?
- What do you see as the main purpose of values?

* * *

धर्म एव हतो हन्ति धर्मो रक्षति रक्षितः ।
तस्माद्धर्मो न हन्तव्यो मा नो धर्मो हतोऽवधीत् ॥

Dharma indeed destroys (those) who destroy it; dharma protects those who protect it. Therefore, dharma should not be destroyed, else dharma that is destroyed will destroy us.

—Manusmriti

CAKE, NOT THE ICING

> *Values are principles and ideas that bring meaning to the seemingly mundane experience of life. A meaningful life that ultimately brings happiness and pride requires you to respond to temptations as well as challenges with honour, dignity, and courage.*
>
> **—Laura Schlesinger**

Why Are We Even Discussing the Subject of Values?

There are various terms which are in use—values, ethics, morals, principles, Code of Conduct, etc. Before we finalize the term we wish to use, let us first understand what we need to achieve, so that we are effective at what we are doing. What term we use in the end really does not matter. What matters is what we do with it to get to where we wish to go.

Let us start from the very beginning. When we look at any organization, what is it that is to be achieved?

Wait! Let us take another step back. Before we get to the organization, let us consider the individual.

When we look at an individual in isolation, does he/she need many rules? Maybe the individual requires some, which the individual chooses to adopt in order to be effective. For the individual to do something in his/her own space, he/she may not worry about so many other factors. He/she will just go ahead and do whatever is to be done.

But the moment that individual comes in contact with other people, be it at home, or in society or at work, we need to consider various aspects of the individual's conduct, behaviour, attitude, etc., because now anything that is to be done is in the presence or context of other individuals.

The moment two or more individuals come together to achieve something, some set of rules, guidelines, decorum, customs, procedures, etc., come into existence. These could be formal, informal, cultural, regional, etc., and could also be written, unwritten, implied, prescribed, etc.

Values, principles, Code of Conduct or anything else you choose to call it is all about that set of whatever which makes a group of individuals more effective, more efficient and more harmonious, at whatever they are doing.

Let Us Explore the Context of a Family

Let us now examine a very familiar space, familiar to each one of us—the family. Here, we have just a few individuals. For this discussion to be meaningful, let us assume at least two members.

If you examine carefully, family is the smallest organizational unit. It is a miniature form, a microcosm of the business organization.

Even in that small organizational unit, we have rules, systems, processes and also values. Just they are not formally identified, shared or documented.

Let us explore the scenario of a typical morning—waking up, sharing the newspaper, making a cup of tea/coffee, using the bathroom, making breakfast, etc.

Do you plan this every day? Did you ever sit down to discuss, how it will all be done? Do you even think about it every day? Do you have a documented procedure manual?

But it all happens, sometimes without even a word being exchanged. Have you ever stopped to wonder how it all happens?

At the foundation of it all, you will appreciate the need for the following:

- Respecting each other's needs
- Understanding each other's personality
- Being flexible, adjusting or adaptable
- Being patient with each other
- Being friendly, cheerful, etc.
- Being punctual

What are these?

Yes, values! Can you imagine the absence of one or more of these? And remember, this is just an hour or so in the morning.

Just imagine, if this is so within the family, that is, with people with whom we share life, what should be the case with people at work, who are not so known to us.

Let Us Move to the Workplace

Take the simple example of a meeting between two individuals that had been decided four or five days in advance. Some of the points that never came up for a discussion or an explicit agreement are as follows:

- Both will be faithful to this arrangement.
- Both will respect each other's normal daily commitments, that is, no one suggested that they meet at 4:00 AM.
- Both understand that the meeting will be in a mutually convenient place.
- Both have faith in the other, and don't need to repeatedly reiterate the date and time commitments.
- Both are open to discussing different options and are flexible.

If we examine such simple commonplace scenarios, in most cases we don't have to explicitly discuss and agree on these points. All these points are implied and there is an implicit understanding between all in a societal context.

Let us now consider the following scenario. A group of individuals are involved in designing of an automobile. Someone has an idea to begin with, and the team has to come up with a design which can be taken to production. Individual A has come from the background of product design, B comes from automobile engineering, C comes from software engineering and so on. There are experts—engineers, designers, etc.—coming from different backgrounds, coming together to make this design a reality.

What is called for here is—how do these people, who came from varied backgrounds, pool in their expertise? Some basic principles (or should we say rules of the game) are required. Each individual has to examine the following:

- Am I open in sharing what I know?
- Am I open in listening to what others have to say?
- Am I respecting others' point of view and ideas?
- Am I contributing to the synthesis of design from the ideas that are being floated?
- Are we all free to debate and argue over whatever differences that arise, and finally arrive at what is needed for that situation?

These and other such understandings are what is required for this team of individuals to come together and arrive at a good design. Needless to say, technical know-how and other such knowledge and expertise are critical for this to happen.

Apart from the technical ingredients which came in as ideas and technical know-how, what made this cohesion happen? What made this team come together? What made a design a reality?

Is that not what values are all about? Or whatever name you chose to call it by.

The aforementioned scenario is in the context of automobile engineering. But the things that make individuals come together and collaborate to achieve the set goals are common, irrespective of departments, organization, industry or even country.

The same holds true for management decisions, where a number of executives of senior management collaborate to take decisions regarding strategy, plan, personnel, etc.

It is almost analogous to a frequency match between individuals. The only point to note is that the frequency match happens at a number of different parameters and levels.

In leadership teams, the right frequency match has to happen. The more that frequency match happens, the more the team is able to meet the objectives of the organization and is also able to go beyond, when required.

One may take the example of a close relationship in the family, say with the father. Even though apparent arguments and disagreements exist, there is a deep understanding between the two individuals—the father and the child.

Yes, it seems nebulous. But as we move to the forthcoming pages of this book, it becomes clear that it is something that can be achieved.

A Natural State to Be in

We all have many tales to tell regarding our experiences—pleasant or unpleasant—in our respective workplaces. Here, we share what a chief financial officer (CFO) of an IT start-up (where the expat founder was based out of Europe) experienced and shared with us.

I was head hunted by a placement firm for an exciting role. It was to be the CFO of a small software products company which had the potential to grow big. The founder explained his plans and shared the vision for growth. I had multiple meetings with the founder and I got convinced of the potential. They needed a senior finance professional to get more funding into the company as venture capital firms wanted good governance and a strong team.

Within three months of joining, I started getting perturbed as I noticed accounting being done under some legal entities which were apart from this company but belonged to the founder. There was a local CEO too for the firm but she was also unaware about this and as she was a marketing person she was never deeply involved with finances.

Whenever I broached this with the founder, I could sense the founder not liking it. The replies were evasive at the best. Even my specific emails were unanswered. The CEO and I jointly tried to have meetings with the founder to get clarity, but this topic was always put aside.

I was hurt and angry. I had left a good job to join this and I felt bad that I was not given a complete and honest picture by the founder and also wasn't given due hearing and felt there was no respect for my concerns as a professional with interests of this organization at heart. I felt cheated. It was stressful. Within 18 months, I left the firm and I still remember, the months I stayed were stressful and not enjoyable at all. The firm also did not do well and never got more funding from other venture capital firms.

Each of us may easily identify with this narration. We almost respond thinking, 'Yes, I too have seen similar demonstrations of lack of integrity, lack of transparency, lack of trust and non-inclusiveness'.

At least one thing is certain through this experience—that we all, at the workplace, expect integrity, openness, trust, inclusiveness, understanding and many other such values. What does this show? A place which resonates with integrity, openness, trust, fairness, etc., seems natural; in other words, that seems like the natural state for us to be in. We are more comfortable being in that setting.

Doesn't that naturalness also show us that values are a natural element in every place where individuals come together? If the environment is devoid of values, we feel uncomfortable.

Pillars of the Organization

Many articles and books regarding business organizations refer to the people (employees), customer and business as three important pillars of every organization. If people are one of the key pillars of an organization, what are the means to strengthening this pillar? When we refer to the term people, we are actually talking about individuals with skills, capabilities, beliefs, character, personality, etc.

The many individuals in the organization become a pillar of the organization when they collaborate harmoniously working towards a common purpose.

What is the building material that brings all individuals together and makes them collaborate? Yes, it is values.

The moment we recognize that the individuals in the organizations are human beings, we can't but give importance to empathy, respect, kindness, trust, camaraderie, etc. What else are these but values, upon which not only the organization but the entire society rests.

Identifying Values: A Simple Example

Consider a team in the accounts department of an organization. On examination, it was revealed that the following aspects contribute to stress among the team members:

- Conflicts with other team members
- Lack of respect from other team members
- Lack of intra-team support to deal with work
- Feeling of being isolated in the team
- Absence of open communication
- Lack of common purpose or goal of the team

Of course, there are other causes for stress among individuals. Let us consider only those that fall in the purview of the team and its members.

Now, ask yourself the following questions:

- Do you identify with these causes of stress in the team?
- Do you believe that the solutions to these causes of stress fall in the context of the team?
- Can we, as a team, identify some steps which, if we put our minds together, will address those aforementioned causes of stress?

On taking up this matter seriously, the team in question in the accounts department came up with the following answers, and in a matter of few months could reduce the extent of stress caused by these factors. The following were the points they implemented in the team:

- Be open in sharing their concerns
- Celebrate milestones

Just introducing these two points had changed the equation among the members of the team, and the members felt that the level of stress owing to the factors mentioned earlier had come down considerably.

What are these two? Do you wish to call them rules? Do you wish to call them principles? Do you want to say this is our way of life? Do you wish to call them rules of the game?

These are nothing but two aspects of interactions about which we have a common understanding as a team.

Whatever name we use for these doesn't matter. Through this book, we would like to introduce the term values.

Other examples of values in this context could be sharing, listening, honesty, etc.

Nice-to-Have or Need-to-Have?

Based on the previous discussions, it is evident that values are not just something that will be nice to have in the organization, to talk about, to write in brochures and to present to clients. It is an essential ingredient for the success and sustenance of the organization.

The significant point to note is that it is already in action. It is just that we don't see it. Just as it is said, the healthy don't know of their health, only the sick do.

The absence of values is easily felt, but the presence of them is never noticed.

Think of the lift you use every day on the way to work. Every component of the lift and the interfaces between all the components are all in perfect order and the lift is functioning properly. You use it every day. But you never notice that it is working perfectly, because the different parts and their interfaces are in perfect order.

Similarly, we never notice that the smooth functioning of a team in the organization is because of the individuals and smooth interactions between them.

The values are like the nuts, bolts, interfaces and lubrications among the various parts in the lift.

In the case of the employees in the organization, if we pay more attention to the interactions between individuals, which is the most foundational element in the organization, we will be able to raise the performance of the organization to a completely different level.

In other words, values ensuring effective interaction between individuals can significantly influence the following:

- Productivity
- Quality
- Innovation
- Creativity
- Excellence

Not only that, values have been known to create an atmosphere where stress is far less, as compared to situations where there is friction amongst the members of the organization.

We shall explore these points in other chapters in this book.

Let us conclude this chapter by presenting what the CEO of LinkedIn, Jeff Weiner, said:

> The flip side is developing a culture with a compassionate ethos. That's what our leadership team has tried to do at LinkedIn; create a culture where people take the time to understand the other person's perspective, and not assume nefarious intention; build trust; and align around a shared mission. After nearly 10 years, I still celebrate the fact we can make important decisions in minutes or hours

that some companies debate for months. Create the right culture, and you create a competitive advantage.

Source: http://knowledge.wharton.upenn.edu/article/linkedin-ceo-how-compassion-can-build-a-better-company/ (accessed on 9 April 2019)

Values in Action—Compassion Even in Crisis

Let us discuss a scenario in a certain organization in the IT services industry, which was shared during one of our discussions with people regarding their experience with values.

At the height of the financial crisis in 2008, lay-offs were being implemented across many organizations in the IT services industry. This organization in question also took the usual route and saw this as an instant remedy to high costs and immediately decided to retrench quite a few of the employees without almost any notice period.

Management had defined certain criteria for the same—cost to company, duration of employment with the company, dispensability to the project, etc. This was applied very mechanically, and most knew that finding a job elsewhere at this juncture would be almost impossible.

Just a day before the rollout, somewhere in the organization, a junior manager in the HR department went beyond these criteria applied to the lay-offs. She went through the employee database and made a list of employees who had taken loans for setting up their homes after a recent marriage or had taken leave on account of childbirth or had medical leave on account of hospitalization of family members, etc.

Though this was resisted by quite a few, this manager stood her ground. Eventually, some saw the compassionate viewpoint in this complicated and extremely tense situation and took her side. Even though it could not be implemented entirely the way she had recommended, but the impact of the sudden lay-off, at least for a few, was mitigated.

Empathy and compassion play an important role in the business organization. It is not that instances of compassion are very rare—just that we do not notice them.

Customer Retention—A Major Benefit

Customers also respect and value the values adopted by your organization. A senior business executive with an IT service organization in India shared the following experience:

> Because of our adherence to values in all transactions, including the ones in the case of customers, we have gained the trust of our customers. We have instances where an overseas customer has told us that if we send an invoice, they don't even have to go through all the details of the invoice to release our payment. That is the extent to which values have helped us in gaining the trust of our customers.

During our study, organizations have shared that their core values which have been nurtured over the years have helped them hugely in customer retention. This is primarily because of the following:

- Due to the consistent values-oriented nature of all the interactions, the customer develops a trust with these organizations.
- The customer finds a great ease in conducting the business.

Here is another experience shared by a senior executive in a manufacturing organization:

> Because of our values, we have been able to establish very good relationships with our vendors as well. For us, where the timely supply of raw materials and their quality is very crucial, relationship with the vendors is extremely critical. A long-term relationship of trust with the vendors also encourages the vendors to invest in systems and processes which benefit our manufacturing operations. Our organization is so particular about our interactions even with the vendors that one relationship manager (of a particular vendor) was asked to resign over an integrity issue. A payment was due to the vendor on a particular date, and the vendor had shown some urgency regarding the same. On the due date (which happened to be a Friday), the relationship manager sent out a communication

to vendor that the payment has been made, even though the accounts team had not been able to initiate the payment. The relationship manager knew of the inability of the accounts department to make the payment, but was eager to get the vendor off his back. The payment could only go through three days later. The management lost no time in taking this particular action. Many organizations would have let this issue pass, or at the most let go of the manager with a minor punishment, but for our organization integrity was important irrespective of who we are dealing with.

A Context for Values in an Organization

While every organization primarily consists of individuals in interaction with each other and the outside world, that may be too oversimplified view. As is evident from Figure 3.1, an organization is not just an entity with a number of individuals, but it is an ecosystem involving many divergent entities, each with its own goals, structure and culture.

Figure 3.1 Context for Values in an Organization

While the organization at the centre (of Figure 3.1) is a collaboration of individuals, each of these other elements that form the ecosystem is also a community of individuals.

While there are rules and regulations that are enforced by industry associations and governments, what helps an organization become successful are its own values.

While it is quite natural to expect that the various entities will have a tendency to pull the organization from different sides, what lends the organization stability and sustenance is values. Values are what keep the organization grounded and anchored within itself, and in the context of the external complexity.

The business interests of the organization's vendors and those of the customers may be divergent, and that may pull the organization into a situation of conflict. The values of the organization are what lend it an identity in the industry, and that is what helps the organization resolve these apparent external conflicts, created by external entities.

For an organization to be successful, it has to take into account the success of all the entities in the ecosystem. If the organization disregards the interest of other entities in the ecosystem, there may be short-term benefits, but in the long term the organization will not be able to survive.

Values Dialogues

Sanjay: I come from a family grounded on strong values, and then again I worked in organizations where being punctual was given a lot of importance. Here, I find that most of the meetings do not start in time, and people walk in at different times. But on the other hand we say values are very important in our culture. How do we reconcile such a situation?

Sheela: (There is a smile on Sheela's face.) First of all, let me acknowledge that this is a conflict we all face from time to time. Here, you are talking about punctuality, but conflicts can arise in other areas as well. I too have faced many such conflicts, and still face them.

Sanjay: Are you saying, this conflict will continue forever? Doesn't sound very nice. What do we do then?

Sheela: I have come to realize—and I am not saying that I have come to the end of my journey—that conflicts are an inevitable and inextricable part of this journey of values. I also believe that the conflicts are like friction in the case of motion. Friction is an integral part of motion.

Sanjay: That sounds very profound.

Sheela: Conflict is also what refines our own conviction regarding values. It fine-tunes our personality and provides courage. Every time I go through a conflict-ridden situation, and emerge at the other end, I feel emboldened by own values-oriented position and feel encouraged to stay on.

Sanjay: If others around are constantly in violation of these values, what is then the motivation for me to continue?

Sheela: I believe that the only reward or benefit of having been values oriented in a particular situation is having been values oriented. Take the simple example of a situation when the help at home falls ill, and out of compassion you take him to the hospital. Is there an assessment of the benefit there? No, you do it because it is your nature to do so. And perhaps at the end you feel good. That's all.

Sanjay: But every time sitting in the conference room and waiting for the meeting to begin, even though we are already 15 minutes late, is very frustrating. And above all, we are always talking of values in the organization. It is a glaring contradiction.

Sheela: I agree, it is. There are two parts to this—one your own adherence to the value of punctuality and the other is what action you are going to take. Regarding your own adherence, it is important that you continue to stay on with it, because that's who you are. Sooner or later, some others, seeing you, will be nudged into that behaviour, at least on some occasions. Another example I talk about often is coming to the signal and stopping first on seeing the red light. Quite often people stop, seeing you stop. Here too in the case of the meeting soon some others will start to come on time, because you are doing so.

Sanjay: Do you think I should also talk to somebody about it?

Sheela: I think that's a good idea. That was the other point I was about to come to. Why don't you take up the issue with the person who called the meeting? Alternatively, if there is the head of the department or the business who is part of the meetings, you can raise it with him or her. I am sure it will have some response. You can also look for a suitable opportunity at the forum to raise it with someone in senior management, since the organization feels that values are important to us.

Sanjay: I will be surprised if there is a solution.

Sheela: Let us give it a shot. It is better than not doing anything. In all such cases, it calls for some patience and perseverance.

Values Reflection

Introspect and deliberate upon these questions as you go forward in strengthening your organization's culture of values:

- What are the values that have ensured smooth functioning of the activities within the boundaries of your family?
- What are the contexts at the workplace where you see the aforementioned values directly relevant and applicable?
- What have been certain situations, in the context of your workplace, where breakdown of values hindered the working of teams?
- Think of a high-performance team in your organization. What are the values that enabled its high performance?
- What are the parallels you see among values between the family and workplace?

***

आ नो भद्राः क्रतवो यन्तु विश्वतः ।

Let noble thoughts come to us from every side.

—Rig Veda

4 | Chapter

CREATIVITY AND INNOVATION

> *Values must come first and must preside over design because they provide the architectonic principles which give aesthetic quality and spiritual coherence to the physical structure embodying the social purpose of institutions.*
>
> **—René Dubos**

Creativity, a term once confined to arts, has now invaded the world of business, abuzz with terms such as competition, disruption, sustainability and globalization. With the aim of creating an edge for themselves over competition, organizations are constantly trying to unleash their creative potential, which is felt to be dormant in their workforce.

'Recruit the best at whatever cost', 'reward the creative minds', 'poach from organizations which are seen as living on the creative edge of technology', 'pick them fresh from ivy league institutes', 'incentivize innovation'—these are certain methods organizations are adopting with a view to instil creativity in their environment. Do these efforts make an organization more creative?

At the same time, people often ask, 'Is it possible to be creative in a business environment?' What does it take to create a culture of creativity in the context of business?

In this chapter, we shall examine how values can play a role in creating an environment that is creative.

Please note that in the context of values, we shall use the terms creativity and innovation interchangeably, and the reason for that will be self-evident as we go through the discussion.

Attributes of Creative Work Cultures

Let us take a moment to examine what Ed Catmull (2014) of Pixar has to say about creativity:

> ...unleashing creativity requires that we *loosen the controls, accept risk, trust our colleagues*, work to *clear the path for them*, and *pay attention to anything that creates fear*.... The way I see it, my job as a manager is to create a fertile environment, keep it healthy, and watch for the things that undermine it.

This experience of Ed Catmull has the following significant points:

- Provide for independence in the team
- Allow members of the team to take risks
- Clear any obstacles in the way of work
- Remove anything that causes threat or fear

Although they seem to be the responsibilities of the leader or manager of the team, these qualities apply to each member of the team. It is very significant that leaders like Ed Catmull almost always lay a lot of stress on the relationships and the interactions among the team members than on the expertise of the individuals in the team.

This is what Lorraine Twohill of Google said:

> Our teams are full of curious, energetic, passionate *people from diverse backgrounds*, and they have *unconventional approaches* to work, play, and life. ...We embrace creativity all around us. *Ideas can come from anyone*, not just a 'Creative' department. We *open-source ideas* internally, and we also *collaborate with many* content creators, artists, developers, brands, agencies, and people who come to us with wonderful ideas.

Source: https://www.thinkwithgoogle.com/marketing-resources/the-curious-case-of-creativity/ (accessed on 9 April 2019)

Pay particular attention to the italicized points.

What does it mean to have 'passionate people from diverse backgrounds' and allow them to have 'unconventional approaches'?

Just imagine having high-performance individuals coming from diverse backgrounds and having their own styles, approaches, viewpoints and idiosyncrasies. It seems like a sure recipe for friction, dramatic meetings, walkouts, etc.

But remember successful organizations in the creative space have been able to harness such diversity and translate it into high levels of creativity and innovation.

Here is what Linda A. Hill of the Harvard Business School says regarding collective genius:

> Innovation usually emerges when diverse people *collaborate* to generate a wide-ranging portfolio of ideas, which they then refine and even evolve into new ideas *through give-and-take* and often *heated debates*. Thus collaboration should involve *passionate disagreement*. Yet the *friction of clashing ideas* may be hard to bear. It *can create tension and stress*—particularly in groups of talented, energetic individuals.

Source: https://hbr.org/2014/06/collective-genius (accessed on 9 April 2019)

Based on these observations, and scanning other success and failure stories of teams engaged in creativity and innovation, it is not difficult to arrive at a list of essential attributes of teams which foster creativity and innovation.

- Collaborative problem-solving
- Individuals from diverse backgrounds
- Trust amongst fellow team members
- Orientation of working for others' success
- Stress-free atmosphere
- Healthy respect for others' views
- Openness to risk-taking
- Healthy and nurturing environment
- Free from threats and fears
- Freedom from the strong clutches of hierarchy and tight control
- Recognition that there will be faults, and mistakes are bound to occur in the path to progress

What Makes This Happen?

Let us examine the first point of the aforementioned list: collaborative problem-solving. Ask two simple questions:

- What makes that happen?
- What are the obstacles to that?

For every answer, again ask yourself the question, 'what makes that possible', and after a few iterations, you will finally arrive at the root causes. This simple exercise will lead us to discover that collaborative problem-solving will not be possible without the values that are the foundation to creativity and innovation among the members of the team, as given below.

- Trust
- Supportiveness
- Integrity
- Empathy
- Flexibility
- Humility

- Patience
- Respect
- Fairness
- Acceptance
- Openness

Here, again we find that the foundation for a team engaged in creative work rests in these values. While experiences are shared using phrases as in the list of essential attributes, let us not forget that what enable these are the values that are the foundation to creativity and innovation.

What Inhibits Creativity?

Like in the case of many other scenarios, it is easy to find many reasons, causes and actions that inhibit creativity in teams. Some of these are as follows:

- Micromanage and create hierarchy-driven management with excessive control
- Push for deadlines. 'I want that creative solution in a week' is a non-starter.
- Being insensitive towards the needs of creative teams: This includes not giving feedback in a manner which acts as a suitable input to further the creative process.

- Manage creativity the way one manages business development, delivery, operations and administration
- Punish failure
- Create systems and procedures that promote fear or threat
- Promote competition amongst individuals and teams
- Create an environment of stress

Creativity and Neuroscience

What does neuroscience say about creativity? Let us consider the instance of laughing at a joke. Psychologists and neuroscientists consider the moment at which we laugh at a joke to be a moment of a creative insight or discovery.

Think of a good joke. Think of occasions when you have laughed at the same. Now think of the ingredients or circumstances required for laughing at the joke and introspect. Could you have laughed at the same joke under times of pressure and stress, or if you were really sad or faced with some personal misfortune? Could you have laughed if you were in a tearing hurry or worried about some goal in mind? Could you have laughed if you were extremely fearful of the consequence?

As you list out all these possibilities, one sees a parallel to circumstances required for a human mind to be creative. Creative idea is like a delicate flower—it blossoms almost magically. It cannot be forced.

Neuroscience points out to default mode network—a brain activity wherein cross-connection of ideas takes place. This network gets to work only when other brain networks dealing with survival or problem-solving subside in their activities. This is entirely in tune with our own personal experience, as in the case of laughing at a joke. Creativity means looking at the world in a newer way to the way we have been viewing and this needs the mind to be able to do that. The default mode getting initiated is an important part of it. The only way to initiate is to ensure the stressors which suppress it—tension, pressure, fear, etc.—are reduced to a large degree.

What Enables Creativity?

In 1926, Graham Wallas proposed a model for creative thinking process (Figure 4.1) as part of his work, titled *The Art of Thought*.

Figure 4.1 Creative Thinking Process	
Saturation	Problem definition and observation
Incubation	Set the problem hidden away and allow the subconscious processing to continue
Illumination	The moment when a new idea breaks through
Verification	Checking to see if the idea actually works

In this abstraction, what is important to note is that while we can assign a time duration to saturation and verification, it is impossible to predict how much time we need to incubate the idea and when that illumination will take place. Both these are not in our direct control.

If it were possible, then Archimedes would not have been in the bath tub when that significant discovery happened!

Why? This is not a deliberate act. This happens in a domain that is beyond our conscious effort and thought process.

This is also illustrated by what Leonardo da Vinci said, 'Men of lofty genius when they are doing the least work are most active'.

Therefore, given that incubation and illumination are beyond our comprehension in terms of measure of time, the creative process cannot be predictably bound by time.

This is not to suggest that it will take a long time. Actually, it could happen in an instant or, at the other extreme, it may not take place at all. While this is true, it is also true that we can significantly increase the odds that the illumination happens more in a reasonable period of time by creating the environment facilitating the same. It is akin to the role a fertilizer plays for a crop—it catalyses and enhances the growth.

While Figure 4.1 attempts to explain the process of creativity in the individual, when it comes to creative teams, the same has to be synchronized at the level of the team, that is, among its members.

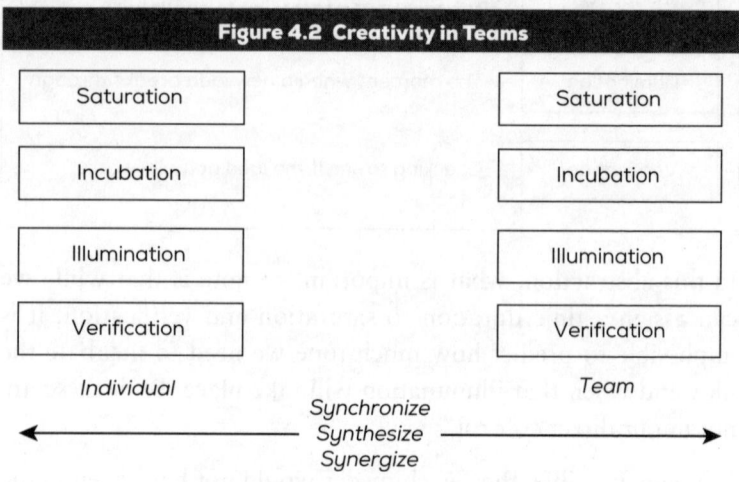

Figure 4.2 Creativity in Teams

In Figure 4.2, one important point to note is that while this applies to individuals as well as teams, the process becomes more complicated when it comes to teams. While understanding that the creative thinking process goes through the afore-mentioned four stages (Figure 4.1), it is equally important to recognize that when it comes to teams, we are dealing with the following three factors:

- Personalities: In any work situation, we are dealing with diverse personalities of individuals and when it comes to creativity, the synthesis of these, at times contrasting individuals, holds the key to bring out the creative best in each.

- Mind: Creativity is an output of the mind, when it is left to its most natural state of expression, as in the case of blooming of a flower. At the most fundamental level, we are dealing with the mind and its intricacies.
- Situations: Understanding the context in which the team is expected to deliver a creative solution is the third crucial factor.

While examining the attributes of creative work cultures, it is evident that for each of these attributes to manifest some fundamental qualities of the human mind need to be in place. This is what we are referring to as values. Values are what provide meaning and purpose to human actions.

For the creative thinking process to be fruitful, the shared values of the teams alone define the success of each of the four stages.

Let us take the example of 'collaboration among individuals from diverse backgrounds' while working towards a creative solution. For this to be real, the following values become critical in these teams:

- Collaboration with trust
- Create and sustain a stress-free atmosphere
- Be supportive of each other's efforts
- Be empathetic
- Be flexible
- Be humble
- Be patient
- Be respectful of each other's views and ideas
- Be fair
- Accept each other for what they are
- Create an environment that nurtures open exchange of ideas
- Have an environment that is free from threats and fears
- Be free from the strong clutches of hierarchy and tight control

Four Core Values of a Design Team

We present here a scenario which most of us would have experienced. Though this particular discussion centres around a team engaged in design of a product, this may be extended to any other problem-solving situation as well. During this discussion, keep the creative thinking process (see Figure 4.1) in mind.

For you to achieve saturation and also allow illumination to happen, you have to be in a state of intense work while being relaxed. Most often we find illumination when we are in a relaxed state, when the mind is free from conventional expectations, wants, threats, fears, etc. The team atmosphere needs to be open, stress-free and relaxed.

So the first core value is be relaxed and contribute to a relaxed and stress-free atmosphere within the team.

As an individual working on a design, whenever you share, with another team member, what you have discovered so far, you would quite often experience the following:

- Greater clarity in what you have come up with
- Some further ideas that you may want to explore further
- Some aha moments when something you had not thought of comes to mind
- Some important feedback to further your work

For these benefits, you have to be prepared to openly share your progress with others. The apprehensions people generally have are as follows:

- I will not get credit for what I have done.
- Someone else will take away the credit.

Just remember, if all great inventors had kept their ideas to themselves, we wouldn't have advanced as a civilization.

So the second core value to cultivate is 'share openly'.

While you share openly, allow others also to do the same and benefit from the sharing. For that, the third core value essential is listen with an open mind, listen with empathy. This allows the others in your team also to benefit from the process of sharing by enhancing each other's ideas.

The aforementioned three values are facilitated if each member of the team believes in the shared purpose of the team—believes that we have to do it together, believes that in others' success is included my success as well. And above all, no member of the team fears that another might take away the credit.

Role of Management

During the process of our study to understand what organizations do to create a culture conducive to creativity, we spoke to an innovation consultant to a large media organization in India who shared this.

I was working with the Vice Chairman of the leading media house in the country. One of their important values is innovative thinking. They have been known to have changed the rules of the business over the decades and have been very successful. This business leader wanted to discuss ways to make the organization look at and nurture new ideas and wanted his executives leading each unit to do the same. In my interaction with him, I realized the reason for this organization to be so successful—he had a tremendous calm within himself—an ability to calmly assess facts without getting distracted and an ability to look deeper into each important issue.

My meetings with him would go for hours—with all distractions kept aside. There wasn't even a clock kept in the room let alone any kind of phone. It was a rare occurrence for us to be disturbed while in a discussion. I noticed that senior executives of the firm knew that one could meet him on a topic only when one was unhurried and not in between rushed activities.

I experienced calmness in my meetings with him. I remember that generation of ideas came spontaneously in that calm setting. It has led me to a deeper appreciation of the quality of mind needed to generate innovative ideas. I appreciate the saying 'you catch heavier fishes in deeper/quieter waters' a lot more now.

This was a clear reinforcement of the point that a quiet, calm mind leads to fresh thinking. Other things the Vice Chairman valued are respect for others' time, provide complete attention to the discussion at hand, allow others to speak freely, provide sufficient time for the meeting, entertain no interruptions during meetings, etc.

It is evident from the previous discussions that it is entirely the responsibility of the management of the teams to create a suitable environment to enable creativity and innovation.

Having recognized the need for the appropriate values in the teams, the management will have to strive to create a values-based culture. Having resolved and committed to build a values-based team, it is the ongoing harmonious interaction between managers and individuals that helps build and sustain an environment of values in the organization.

The following factors are critical to building of a values-based culture, in addition to the points already discussed earlier:

- Unflinching commitment and demonstration of values by the management
- Open exchange of ideas and feedback between the employees and the management
- Transparency in decision-making

Values Dialogues

Sanjay: I am leading a team where we are engaged in design. We are so inundated with here-and-now problems like team stability, long working hours, etc., how do we come up with creative solutions?

Sheela: Can you elaborate that a bit? Can you elaborate the point about team stability?

Sanjay: Recently, one person resigned, and two have been reassigned to another project. As a result, we have lost some experience from our team. And the knowledge transfer could not be done to our satisfaction. I understand we couldn't do much in the case of the person who resigned, but the case of reallocation of personnel to another project was unacceptable.

Sheela: Did you enquire why the reallocation of those two happened, or did anyone explain to you before doing it?

Sanjay: No. I was just informed of the change. I am quite miffed by this, and the entire team is feeling almost cheated.

Sheela: I understand. I feel you should try and find out why this happened. Driven by specific needs, there are occasions when one does reassign responsibilities within the team. But you should have had information and time to plan and execute this change.

Sanjay: As a result of all this, we are having to put in long hours to make up for the losses. And the net result, creativity suffers. We are not able to come up with solutions that will help the design we had in mind. When someone talks of values at this juncture, it is quite frustrating. What is the best way of dealing with this situation?

Sheela: I agree with you. There is no point of talking of values at this time. Let's see what needs to be done. Also, it has to be done within the context of the team. When you examine the situation carefully, the only ones who can do anything about it are the members of the team. So what is it that each of us needs to bring to the table to achieve what we have to? What do you expect from each of your members, and from yourself, to sail over this situation?

Sanjay: First, set aside what has happened and move on.

Sheela: Yes, in all such situations, one thing that immediately helps is not thinking about what has happened and move on. You will also agree that it is not the hard skills that matter at this juncture. Because all the members of the team are sufficiently skilled, I assume. What matters is how the members of the team come together.

Sanjay: What does coming together mean?

Sheela: I am glad you asked that question. Coming together means how harmoniously the entire team collaborates, setting aside differences and conflicts, believing in the shared purpose. The shared purpose in challenging times often works wonders. When it comes to brass tacks, it is about respecting each other's ideas and views, not hesitating to provide your inputs, helping each other, supporting each other in the different tasks and so on.

Sanjay: (Smiling) You have gone one full circle and come back to values.

Sheela: Isn't that what human interaction is all about, Sanjay?

Sanjay: Can't refute that.

Values Reflection

Introspect and deliberate upon these questions as you go forward in strengthening your organization's culture of values:

- What are possible reasons that creativity or innovation has failed to establish ground in your team?
- What are the values demonstrated by your team that can enable innovation in your team performance?
- What are the values that your team needs to inculcate so as to become more effective in collaborative problem-solving?
- What were the situation(s), in hindsight, where had there not been too much pressure from the management, you could have been more creative?
- How often have you seen threats or fears among team members impact their creative instincts? Describe the situations and the problems created by threats and fears.

* * *

यत्रोऽत्साहसमारम्भः यत्रालस्यविहीनता ।
नयविक्रमसंयोगः तत्र श्रीरचला ध्रुवम् ॥

Where there is perseverance in the effort, where there is an
absence of idleness, where there is a union of humility and
courage, there sustained success and prosperity are certain.

—Subhaashitam

5 AND 5
BECOME 50

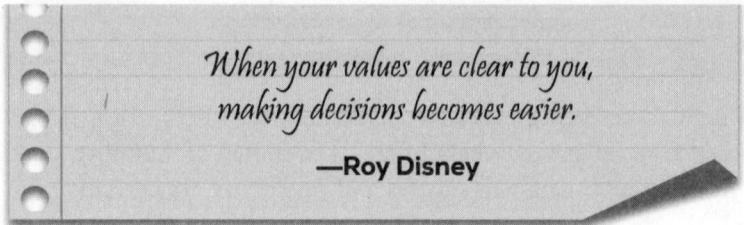

When your values are clear to you, making decisions becomes easier.

—Roy Disney

The idea of instilling values in an organization is not for the sake of values or being seen as values based, but to create an environment of high productivity, excellence, innovation and creativity. Above all, values also create an environment which minimizes stress, about which we shall discuss in the next chapter.

Any such initiative will make sense in the context of a business organization only when both the organization (i.e., the business) and the employees as individuals stand to benefit. These benefits, discussed across this book, have been summarized in Table 5.1.

Table 5.1 Benefits of Values: Organizational and Individual	
Organization	**Individual**
• Business success • High productivity • Quality • Culture of innovation • Creative mindset • Sustainability • Stress-free environment • Low attrition	• Individual excellence • High productivity • Low stress levels • Well-being at work

For the idea of values to be purposeful in an organization, it has to contribute to achievement of the goals of the organization, in other words to the objective of its very existence. In this chapter, we shall discuss and analyse the idea of performance (in terms of productivity, excellence, quality) and see how here again values are the very foundation of these.

An Organization Is about Teamwork

'It's all about teamwork'. We hear this quite often at work. Let us first examine what a team is. According to BusinessDictionary.com, a team is

> a group of people with a full set of complementary skills required to complete a task, job or project. Team members (a) operate with a high degree of interdependence, (b) share authority and responsibility of self-management, (c) are accountable for the collective performance, and (d) work towards a common goal and share rewards.

It is easy to identify and induct individuals with complementary skills into a team. But the challenge lies in harnessing that complementariness to create an effective, productive, creative and excellent team.

What makes a set of individuals function as a team? Values.

When teams are driven by values, their performance far exceeds the sum of individual performances—resulting from the harmony and synergy resulting from the values-oriented culture prevailing in the teams.

In the article 'The Secrets of Great Teamwork', Haas and Mortensen (2016) discuss the following as enablers of high performance in teams: compelling direction, strong structure, supportive context and shared mindset. The authors go on to stress that while direction, structure and support are important, it is the ability to collaborate and synthesize capabilities based on the existing diversity that enables high performance in teams.

The team is able to collaborate effectively and harness that complementariness only when there is a culture of trust, flexibility, respectful exchange of ideas and coexistence of multiple points of view without conflict.

Amy Edmondson, Professor of Leadership and Management at the Harvard Business School, describes three pillars of team culture as curiosity, passion and empathy.

Productivity

Let us begin this discussion by examining the experience shared by a young team member in a BPO organization.

> We were a team of around 10 members in this project. We were nearing a crucial deadline, and we had about two weeks to go for completing the project. Many of us worked long hours, and one of us was even unwell during this time. In spite of her poor health, she spent extra hours, and we finally managed to complete the project on time to the client's satisfaction. Some days later that same person (the lady who was unwell) had some family commitments, and came late to work by about an hour or so on two to three occasions. The manager said it was not okay and logged it as a half-day leave. Not only I, but the entire team, was shaken by the incident. Some of the younger members of the team were very affected by it and said that they will not spend extra hours at work, even if the situation demanded. This also brought down the productivity and quality of performance of the team in that particular project.

This is a striking example of a situation where a certain attitude and action resulted in loss of productivity and quality of the team. In this case, it was the outcome when a manager conducted himself in a manner that the employees saw as unfair and un-empathetic. Many of us may have experienced various situations in our career where certain decisions or actions resulted in dampening the enthusiasm at work, resulting in lowering of productivity and quality.

When youngsters face such instances early on in their career, they leave a lasting impact on their approach towards work.

We would like you to ponder over the following question in a similar situation that might have occurred in your organization:

How does the organization then gain the trust and loyalty of such disgruntled employees?

This recovery indeed is a very tough thing. It takes a lot of time, effort and sensitivity to regain the trust and commitment of employees who feel that they have been treated in an unfair manner.

The subject of productivity can be discussed in various ways. After the following discussion, you may want to apply the same line of thinking to the idea of productivity as has been adopted in your organization.

To explore the idea of productivity here, we refer to the idea of employee engagement as described in the 'pyramid of employee needs' (Garton and Mankins 2015).

The authors state that 'If satisfied employees are productive at an index level of 100, then engaged employees produce at 144, nearly half again as much. But then comes the real kicker: inspired employees score 225 on this scale'.

Who is an engaged employee? Following are the factors which facilitate engagement[1]:

- Greater involvement
- High level of commitment
- Perception of the job importance
- Clarity of expectations
- Regular dialogue with superiors
- Working relationship with peers, superiors, subordinates
- Perception of ethos and values of the organization
- Transparency in the environment

While all these factors apply to the individual, these are not enabled by the individual alone. The collective effort as a team becomes important here.

---

[1]This list is indicative. Different organizations may define employee engagement differently based on the context and their business needs.

What-Enables-It Analysis

For each of these factors, suppose you ask the question 'what enables it', and you continue to ask the question 'what enables it', till you are not able to break it down any further, you will realize that you have reached the values that enable all these.

Let us take the first factor in the list as an example: greater involvement. A segment of this analysis is presented as follows:

What enables greater involvement?

- Clarity of work definition
- Shared purpose in the team
- Freedom to perform
- The team management and the organization repose trust in the individual

What enables freedom to perform?[2]

- The manager respects the decisions of the team members.
- The manager trusts the individuals.
- There is an environment of collaboration in the team.
- The manager is not breathing down the neck all the time.
- The individual is not constantly reminded of the threats of non-performance.

What enables an environment of collaboration?[3]

- The team members trust each other.
- There is mutual respect for each other's points of view.
- There is mutual respect for each other's capabilities.
- There is greater flexibility among the team members to adapt to situations.
- There is transparency among the team members.[4]

---

[2]Similar exercise can be done for the other points mentioned before.
[3]Similar exercise can be done for the other points mentioned before.
[4]Certainly, you may come up with different sets for your own organization, but this exercise will give you the idea of what we are trying to communicate.

This exercise can be carried out for each of the enablers of greater involvement and can be followed through till it cannot be broken down any further. This exercise is similar to performing root-cause analysis, where we drill down to finding out the root causes.

Here, since we are trying to arrive at the fundamental enablers, we have called it the what-enables-it analysis.

If you examine the last set of bullet points, you will notice that we come down to the following values: trust, respect, flexibility and transparency.

What does this demonstrate? For anything to happen in the organization, if we drill down to fundamental enablers, these will turn out to be what we have been calling values.

Based on this what-enables-it analysis, we are able to understand the importance of values in facilitating engaged employees.

Inspired Employee

A corporate planning executive for one of India's leading IT training and software services companies shared the following:

I was a fresh recruit direct from college, recruited for a planning role. I remember my very second day in office, post our induction. My manager had called me and told me to come with him to a meeting. It was a senior business planning meeting of the software products division with all the business leaders present. I was introduced to the group and asked to attend the meeting and be an active part of it. My manager later asked me for my opinion on some things discussed.

I felt really happy. I remember feeling engaged with my work and looking back I feel that the reason was the experience of being treated as a thinking person and valued for my opinions and not letting hierarchy-based behaviour be the norm. This also I think influenced the way I worked with people throughout my career. I knew that not all managers were like this—some of my friends worked with others who were very seniority-based and wore their rank up the sleeve.

That was an example of how being respected, listened to and being trusted had a phenomenal impact on the newcomer.

What makes an employee an inspired one?

When the organization is small, each one of the employees seems charged, motivated and inspired. The following are some of the key reasons for that:

- Shared dreams
- Feel a part of the vision
- Open and transparent
- Trust in each other to fulfil that dream
- Mentally prepared for all the challenges

Yes, capabilities are important; intellectual properties are important; ideas and strategies are important—but what make it all happen are the people. And what make the people come together in an inspired way? *It is the shared dreams, the shared purpose, the shared values.*

Performance = Potential – Interference

W. Timothy Gallwey, in his book *The Inner Game of Tennis*, said that your performance equals your potential minus your interference. He said that various factors such as fears, imagination, fantasy and self-doubt get in the way of your performance. In other words, to realize your potential, you must minimize the interfering thoughts in your mind.

What are the various interferences? Following are some, based on responses we had from some employees we spoke to:

- Lack of appreciation of reality
- Conflicts with other members in the team
- Inability to adapt to changing context
- Inability to accept feedback
- Lack of trust in others in the team

- Threats from supervisor (perceived or otherwise)
- Task is challenging (beyond skill level)
- Insufficient time to perform to given task
- The task depends on others and there is not enough cooperation from others (peers, subordinates, seniors)
- High expectation from others regarding the task
- Disturbing work environment (not conducive to work)
- Impromptu meetings with co-workers—distraction

Of course, depending on the organization, department, team or situation at hand, the list of inhibitors that affect performance can be very varied. Broadly speaking, these can be classified into the following:

- Individual factors
- Team factors
- Project/department factors
- Organizational culture factors

You will agree that these factors are not beyond human control. While, in a particular context, it is possible that some of these factors cannot be avoided, with the support from the team and organization, the impact of these factors can certainly be mitigated.

In our conversations with employees from across different organizations, it has been found that employees feel that the following within the team members can greatly help in eliminating, or at least mitigating, the impact of these factors:

- Support of the team in difficult situations
- Transparency within the team
- Respect for each other
- Empathy
- Appreciation for everyone's efforts

With just these values being present within the team, a large set of interferences can be mitigated, thereby enhancing the performance of the individual, the team and hence the organization.

Values are the key ingredient in mitigating the
interferences in the organization, and hence
key to enhancing performance.

Pillars of Quality

The quality movement across the world began more than half a century ago. Quality standards and frameworks dominated the scene. Every organization spent enormous amount of effort and money to implement quality management systems across the organization.

Every organization, in its attempt to define its quality improvement programme, defined its quality policy and also communicated its intent through its pillars of quality. Invariably most organizations stated that their people and systems/processes were two of their important pillars in this framework (Figure 5.1). Depending on the culture of the organization, other pillars included customer focus, empowerment, leadership, etc.

But that is not what we are trying to stress upon here. Let us turn our attention to the foundation of all these pillars. Most organizations realized that the foundation of these pillars was strengthened by the organization's values.

Figure 5.1 Pillars of Quality

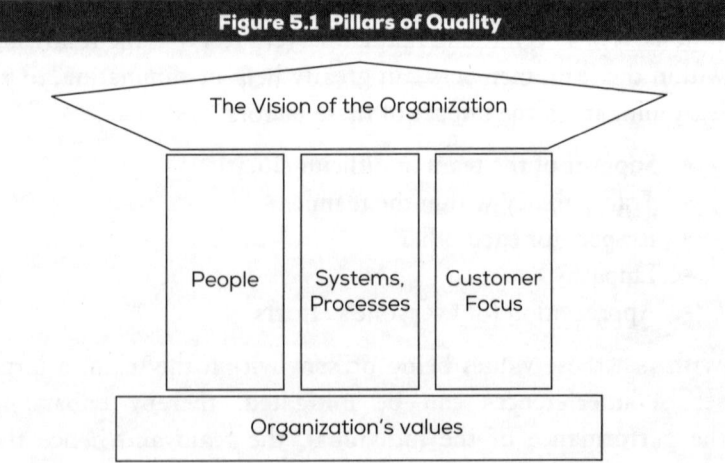

The Vision of the Organization

People | Systems, Processes | Customer Focus

Organization's values

Good Values, Great Business

Going beyond the foundation, most organizations identified people and processes as their pillars.

In any organization, when you say people, what are you essentially referring to? Yes, you are referring to the values that people embody.

When we refer to processes, let us not forget that people are what enable processes.

What does that mean? Values are the key. They are the foundation.

Values Dialogues

Sanjay: During our last project, in the final stages, many of the members of our team had to work late hours and they did a great job of completing the project on time. But on certain occasions, some of them could not come to work at the usual time of 9 AM, and the automated system logged them as late and in some cases—as per articulated policy—tagged them in for half-pay for that day. In such a scenario, are not our own systems and processes in conflict with our intention of creating a culture of values, where employees respect and honour their commitment to the customer?

Sheela: That's indeed a complex situation. Systems and processes are implemented in any organization for facilitating smooth functioning and effectiveness, and ultimately to serve the objectives of the organization. The systems and processes need to take into account cultural elements of the workplace.

Sanjay: What does that mean?

Sheela: Let us take the case of a department that caters to customers in another time zone. It is understandable that the employees engaged in that project will try and follow some timings that will suit that customer, say in order to have a live video conference. In such a scenario, the attendance system has to cater to flexibility in timings. This, of course, is a very straightforward case.

Sanjay: I was just about to say that. What about the cases where a certain amount of flexibility is required?

Sheela: I completely agree with you. We do have employees who respond to the call of situations, where we have tight deadlines, or other such challenging circumstances where extra effort is called for. These employees are demonstrating values such as commitment, sincerity, loyalty, etc. And all organizations are founded on such values, which often are not talked about. In such cases, it is the responsibility of the organization to reciprocate, by demonstrating values such as trust, fairness, empathy and integrity. If the organization fails to do so, then the employees lose their faith in the organization resulting in low morale. And that could translate into low productivity and lower quality output.

Sanjay: Also creativity is compromised. I have always found that, in the absence of enthusiasm, we may end up completing the tasks, but the expected level of excellence is not to be seen in the work.

Sheela: True. In a way, you can see that values at the individual level complement the values from the organization's side. Actually, the latter also comes from individuals alone, only that they are perceived by every individual to come from the organization.

For example, you say I am loyal to the organization and I expect the organization to trust me. What does it mean to say 'organization should trust me'? The organization doesn't do that. It is individuals again. In some cases, what we refer to as the organization is the senior management, which again is a team of individuals.

In conclusion, what I would like to say is when the organization has some expectations from the employee, the organization has some responsibility towards the employee and vice versa.

This is probably at the very core of the whole idea of values— *whenever we have an expectation from anybody, we have a responsibility towards that individual.*

Values Reflection

Introspect and deliberate upon these questions, in the context of your organization, as you go forward in strengthening your organization's culture of values:

- Perform the what-enables-it analysis for improving productivity in your immediate team.
- Think of your immediate team. What are the attributes of the team that makes it a cohesive and effective team? Do you find these attributes present in all the teams across the organization?
- In your organization, what are the values that strengthened the quality improvement programme? In other words, which values in the organization contributed to the culture of quality?
- Do you classify your team as consisting of engaged employees or inspired employees? Why?
- What values, if adopted by your team, will transform the members of your team into engaged employees?

***

मैत्री करुणामुदितोपेक्षाणां सुखदुःखपुण्यापुण्यविषयाणां
भावनातश्चित्तप्रसादनम् ।

Friendliness towards the happy, compassion towards unhappy, delight towards good and unbiasedness towards bad lead to undisturbed calmness of the mind.

—Patanjali Yoga Sutra

6 Chapter

PATH TO WELL-BEING

> *Work and play are words used to describe the same thing under differing conditions.*
>
> **—Mark Twain**

Studies show that suicides related to work are on the rise internationally. *Newsweek* in its August 2016 publication 'Workplace Suicides Are Rising and Globalization Is to Blame', by Sarah Waters and Jenny Chan stated, 'Studies in the United States, Australia, Japan, South Korea, China, India and Taiwan all point to a steep rise in suicides in the context of a generalized deterioration in working conditions'.

Most suicides can be linked to pressures from economic downturn, lay-offs at work and stress caused at workplace.

Nowadays, whenever you discuss work-related matters with anyone, the conversation sooner or later comes to the subject of stress. Most employees seem to be taking home two things—a pay check and stress.

According to ASSOCHAM, nearly 42.5 per cent of employees in private sectors are afflicted with depression or general anxiety disorder. All this is attributed to demanding schedules, high stress levels and performance-linked perquisites. Data from Optum indicates that 46 per cent of the workforce in organizations in India suffers from some or the other form of stress. Some studies show that almost three-fourths of the employees believe that stress levels have gone up substantially over the last generation.

A study in 2016, in United Kingdom, showed more than 45 million working days had been lost due to stress, anxiety and depression in the past three years, and last year alone, the cost to the economy was at least £2.4 billion. Studies from the USA indicate that between 40 per cent and 60 per cent of the workforce experience stress at the workplace.

These data from affluent economies indicate that high stress levels at the workplace are becoming quite a universal phenomenon.

Stress and Health

The problem of stress does not stay as mere complaints from the workforce. It has been established by medical professionals that stress manifests itself as physical disorders at the bodily level. It is now a very common experience. Here are some of the common bodily disorders, which are attributed to stress, among other causes: heart disease, asthma, obesity, diabetes, headaches, depression and anxiety, gastrointestinal problems, Alzheimer's disease, accelerated aging, premature death, etc.

Stress Impacts Productivity

In the presence of stress, there is no doubt that any individual's output is not going to be up to the usual standards. Everybody will vouch for this. The fact that stress negatively impacts productivity has been proven by numerous researchers.

Some business organizations have created facilities or services to take care of household needs of employees, like payment of bills, help with school admission of children, etc. These organizations recognize that if an employee is bogged down by these things, then obviously it is going to impact the frame of mind, which will affect different activities at the workplace also. Organizations have realized that even marginally easing such pressures can have substantial impact on the comfort level of employees, which in turn affects the quality of output.

Search for a Solution

With the problem so rampant, everyone today is seeking to redress stress. Stress management, meditation and mindfulness programmes, spiritual retreats and vacations are among the very popular methods today.

Here, in this book, we endeavour to go beyond these and discuss how the most natural solutions to dealing with stress lie in values.

What Is Stress?

Is there a need to define the term stress? At a functional level, it is a universally understood word, almost like the word happy. When someone says, 'I am stressed', we don't ask 'what do you mean by that'. The cause of stress may be varied, but the effect is generally understood.

According to the Oxford dictionary, stress is 'a state of mental or emotional strain or tension resulting from adverse or demanding circumstances'. Stress is a 'condition when there is a gap between what the situation demands and the individual's mental ability to address it'.

In certain situations, there is a gap between 'the individual's perception of what is' and 'the individual's expectation in that context', viewed with respect to the individual's ability. When the gap is negative, not in favour of the individual, there is stress. By stress we mean the negative connotation of the word stress. Doing something meaningful and exciting also causes our adrenalin to get activated and we feel a positive stress, but in the context of this book and this chapter in particular, we are referring to the negative and detrimental aspects of stress—those which cause harm to us.

Causes of Stress to the Individual

While most people discuss solutions to stress at the individual level, it is important to understand that there are various non-individual factors which can be influenced by the members of any team which can hugely help in reducing stress levels. For this, let us first understand the causes of stress at the workplace.

For the convenience of understanding and also finding a solution, let us capture the causes of stress in the following six categories:

- Individual (personal) factors
- Individual (organizational) factors
- Family life factors
- Immediate team factors
- Supervisor/manager factors
- Organizational culture, systems and policies-related factors

Note that the categorization can be done in various ways, but we have chosen one where we are able to identify triggers that can help in mitigating stress levels.

Based on the survey we conducted across different kinds of organizations, across different industries, the following is an indicative list of causes of stress in each of the categories. Take time to ponder over each and tick against each that you think is adding to your current stress level.

• Individual (Personal) Factors
  o Individual's personality (individual's worldview)
  o Health (there could be a cause-and-effect relationship here)
  o Sleeping habits (there could be a cause-and-effect relationship here)
  o Diet and eating habits
  o Aspirations and ambitions
  o Fears (real and imagined)
	• Immediate Team Factors
	  o Conflicts with other team members
	  o Lack of respect/recognition from team
	  o Poor work relationship
	  o Feeling of being isolated
	  o No open communication
	  o Lack of support from team in addressing problems regarding work

• Individual (Organizational) Factors
  o Ambiguity/conflict in role/responsibility
  o Unable to manage subordinates (task allocation/management)
  o Poor relationships with boss
  o Workload
  o Deadline pressure
  o Performance targets beyond reach
	• Supervisor/Manager Factors
	  o Micromanagement
	  o Lack of transparency
	  o Non-flexible management style
	  o Autocratic management style
	  o Absence of empathy, compassion
	  o Listening deficiency

• Family Life Factors
  o Strained relationships in the family
  o Strained financial position
	• Organizational Culture, Systems and Policies-Related Factors
	  o Lack of job security
	  o Not sure of future at the job
	  o Promotion or demotion or stagnation related

○ Worry over children and their achievements (or lack of) ○ Worry over health of self, parents, spouse, children, siblings ○ Lack of time at home (including sleep) ○ Lack of strong social circle/ involvement	○ Lack of transparency in decisions ○ Poor physical work environment ○ Lack of transparency

If you have more than 10 ticks, reflect on which ones could be reduced. Similarly if you are a team leader, think from a team member's perspective. These factors are interrelated: every tick here adds up non-linearly, that is, one of the factors in family life may impact the individual's behaviour at work or vice versa.

Needless to say, the aforementioned list is only an indicative list of items that can cause stress to any individual. There is no clear rule to what causes stress to an individual. A situation that causes stress to one individual may be a positive stimulus to another. Here are some examples:

- Some individuals are comfortable being micromanaged, while to some others the situation may be stressful.
- Lack of information causes stress to some, while more information causes stress to some.

The head of the structural division of a leading steel plant shared that he was conscious of the stress levels in the manufacturing industry. He made it a point to ensure that he spoke to each of his staff regularly to enquire about their well-being. According to us, this might be one of the reasons his unit has high employee engagement levels and lower levels of staff turnover.

What Do Our Own Experiences Say?

All of us have had situations at the workplace where, working on the most challenging projects, we experienced no stress; we rather enjoyed working in those projects and recall those experiences fondly.

At the same time, we have had experiences where even though we were part of simple straightforward activities, we encountered very stressful moments during the course of that project.

We will do well to introspect over both these specific situations regarding what happened and why it happened? You will be surprised to find that such introspections yield deep insights into the causes of stress and that of stress-free environments.

Here's what a team leader said, who had been recently promoted to the position in an IT services company:

> I was just a few months into my new role and was still learning and getting acquainted with my new responsibilities. I was definitely under some stress. I had also recently got married and moved in with my husband's family. It was a period of stress on the home front too. When I returned to work after my leave, following the wedding, I was certainly quite stressed. I had a meeting with my boss, the senior project manager, in order to get back into the project work, and I had hinted about the situation at home. Beginning the very next day, I received so much support from my boss and also from the members of the team that I soon became comfortable with my new role and did well too. It also helped me address the situation at home and soon everything was quite peaceful, both at home and at work.
>
> It was a very empathetic response from my boss and the team that helped me to be soon free of the stress I was experiencing at work and home. Because of the empathy and support, I could easily settle into my new role. It was a great lesson that taught me to be sensitive to each individual's personal needs, so that to the best possible extent we can attempt to support him/her in that time of pressure from different quarters.

We are sure that you have had similar situations at the workplace.

What Role Can Values Play to Reduce Stress?

In most of the conversations we had with organizations, values were seen only as something that is nice to have. People feel that it is right to talk about it. The following was another interesting observation: 'as the organization becomes well known, the management feels compelled to use the "values-related" vocabulary in all its communications'. In other words, it uses 'politically correct-sounding words' whenever it is addressing an audience, with regards to values.

And in such a scenario, when people see that the talk and the walk do not match, they feel very disillusioned and start to feel convinced that values and business don't go together.

Are values really beneficial? That's the question people often raise.

Typically, this is the proximate causal mindset people have.

But interestingly, whenever we have asked executives which portion of their long careers they enjoyed the most, they inevitably point out to a time when they experienced at least one or more of the following: an empowered environment, a challenging time with support given, a time when they felt valued and respected, a time when it was fun working with others and all had shared goals and aspirations. This has been across industries and even cultures.

Yet another question when asked almost always provides a negative answer: Tell us an organization/institution bereft of any strong values but successful over sustained period of time? As contra examples, sometimes, they quote organizations which are successful but are palpably short on some important values, but in each case the person being asked also comes up with a list of values these organizations strongly adhere to. An executive recently shared an example of an organization he grudgingly likes—as it doesn't resonate with some important values he cherishes—but he also shared that the same organization values entrepreneurship and empowers people to think big.

If we look at our daily life in the context of the family and society, and even the workplace, there are enough and more examples of values at work.

Take the case of our family life. When we come into the family-fold, there is a lot of peace, quiet and also absence of stress.

Yes, there would be instances when stress does show up, but we also have systems in place which help us counter that stress. There is a need to examine why that is the case?

In most cases, when we come home to our family, we find a sense of peace there. Have you ever wondered why? Where does the peace come from?

It comes because of some fundamental values that are upheld in the context of the family. Perhaps we don't call it values; perhaps we don't call it anything. But there is something—whether we call it values, principles, our family culture, etc. Also, it is so naturally all-pervading.

For example, most often with the kind of communication we have at home, we talk things out. And problem is solved quite often. So stress is reduced.

There is a lot of openness at home, at least relatively, as opposed to at the workplace. We don't hide anything from each other, or at least it is far less. We feel we have the freedom to say what we want. Above that, there is a love, compassion, etc. That is why that environment becomes comforting, peaceful and above all has much less stress.

What Role Can the Organization Play in Reducing Stress?

Organization's raison d'etre is success and accomplishing stated objectives. Organizations are driven by goals and in today's environment the goals seem to get more ambitious. A recent article by Lee and May (2018) showed the stress of overwork in Korea leading to deaths necessitating urgent social intervention at the policy level. So do big hairy audacious goals cause stress?

Most organizations seem to accept stress as a necessary component or as a natural offshoot of the kind of work they engage in. Seldom do they engage in a conscious effort to address stress as a problem or challenge by itself.

In all our conversations, job content alone seldom came out as the primary cause of stress at the workplace. Usually, the culprit is the larger environment within the organization. We have seen teams with larger, more ambitious goals working under lesser stress.

Apart from recognizing the impact of stress (in individuals) on productivity, quality and other business parameters, some business organizations across the world are also appreciating the importance of well-being of individuals while at work, introducing mindfulness and other such approaches to counter stress.

If we examine the list of factors that can cause stress to the employee, the solution is apparent. Let us revisit each of the six categories (of stress-causing factors) and explore what role the organization can play in addressing the different factors to mitigate stress.

- Individual (personal) factors: Here, the causes are very personal to the employee and are beyond the purview of the employer. But some organizations are taking interest in some of the aspects by supporting the employee in the areas of health, organizing programmes on personal well-being, stress management workshops, meditation, self-improvement workshops, etc. Some organizations even make it mandatory for employees to take annual vacations, as a means to rejuvenation.

  While these initiatives (which are one-time activities) have their impact in helping the employees deal with stress, the effect is short-lived. The effect wears off sooner or later. This is where creating a work culture that is stress-free goes a long way towards addressing individual well-being.

- Individual (organizational) factors: Majority of what are called work stress factors due to organizational factors can be addressed by the manager or the supervisor of the individual. These depend on the management style or culture in the organization. Application of the following values by the manager/supervisor can have a huge impact in mitigating the stress caused: compassion, teamwork, trust, empathy, patience, fairness, transparency and flexibility.

- Family life factors: This category clearly falls in the personal space of the employee, and almost all individuals do not like or expect any interference from the organization in this regard. However, there are organizations which organize personal improvement workshops, which have been known to help individuals manage problems in family life better. They also have activities which involve the family members.

- Immediate team factors: This is also one area where values have been found to have a very high impact in reducing stress levels.

It has been seen that most high performance teams also exhibit low stress levels. This is primarily because the values that enhance collaboration and effectiveness within the team leading to high performance are also the values that enable individuals to support each other and that support often extends beyond the boundaries of work.

Values like compassion, empathy, transparency, flexibility, trust, teamwork, etc. have been seen to be attributes of high performance. At the same time, individuals are keen to become part of such teams where these values are very prominently active. Employees also say that it is most fun to be part of such teams. Fun does not indicate parties, outings, etc., but it is an indicator of very low stress levels.

Our studies showed that teams where people are highly effective as well as engaged, both in mind and spirit, might not have always identified these values as something of a foundation for these teams. But a closer examination of these teams will reveal that these values are what form the basis for all functions and interactions.

In some cases, you might find that there are a few individuals who dominate the functioning of these teams who have these qualities, and that has a rub-off effect on the teams and they show up in the activities and outcomes of these teams.

The nature and degree of stress in teams differ according to the nature of work, leadership, team composition, skill and capability levels, etc. It may be essential to pay special attention to specific teams to provide relief from stress.

- Supervisor/manager factors: Travis Bradberry, co-author of the book *Emotional Intelligence 2.0*, said: 'More than half of people who leave their jobs do so because of their relationship with their boss'. Some may state the same in this manner: 'I would have continued in the same organization, but for my boss'.

While engaging in coaching and counselling engagements, we have seen that there is a very high correlation between an executive's relationship between his/her immediate seniors and the perceived stress levels.

For many who continue in the same place for whatever reasons, they feel it is a very stressful existence.

What is the solution? Rather, what is a way to prevent such situations? Travis Bradberry adds: 'Smart companies make certain their managers know how to balance being professional with being human. These are the bosses who celebrate an employee's success, empathize with those going through hard times, and challenge people, even when it hurts'.

It all begins with empathy—the ability to understand or vicariously experience the feelings or thoughts of another. For a manager, this ability is the backbone of his/her role.

In their *Harvard Business Review* article, Zenger and Folkman (2014) list out the competencies that were voted the most important for all management positions. Among these are values such as 'inspires and motivates others' and 'collaborates and promotes teamwork'.

For these competencies to be demonstrated, the manager has to live the following values: integrity, honesty, compassion, trust, empathy, patience, fairness, transparency, sincerity and flexibility.

- Organizational culture, systems and policies-related factors: Examine the causes of stress that had been listed earlier in this chapter under the heading 'Organizational culture, systems and policies-related factors'. It does not require any major analysis to conclude that it is most crucial for every organization to establish and sustain a culture of values.

At the foundation of it all, every organization has to cultivate the following values, across all levels: transparency in decisions, respect for individuals and their views, integrity, freedom to express, trust, non-discrimination (on the basis of gender, race, religion or colour).

Almost every final year student we have interacted with has shared that the reason he/she has an organization in his/her desired list of organizations to work for is primarily the culture he/she would like to work in. This was also a pleasant surprise to us as we expected compensation and perks to be the most quoted reason. And it is no coincidence that these cherished organizations are known for many of the aforementioned values.

Values Dialogues

Sanjay: We are constantly faced with stretch goals here. As a result, we are always under stress, and some have contracted health issues as well. Is it mission impossible to have stretch goals and at the same time have an environment of well-being and fun?

Sheela: Let us remember that we are all spending much of our wakeful hours every day at work, and any stress we create here, we carry it into the home front. So let us do whatever we can to avoid creating stress here. Now, tell me, have you worked with stretch goals in the past?

Sanjay: Yes.

Sheela: Were you stressed in all the cases of stretch goals?

Sanjay: No.

Sheela: So we are clear that stretch goals by themselves are not causing the stress. Let us think about those past experiences and see what was present in those projects and situations where you had worked with stretch goals and still worked without stress. Do you remember why?

Sanjay: I remember this one project where in spite of the stretch goals, there was something whereby we were all enjoying those challenges and had fun.

Sheela: So not only were you not stressed, but also had fun, in spite of the stretch goals. What made that happen? Did you not feel the pressure of deadlines?

Sanjay: Yes, we had the pressures. But we were all together as a team. We all felt that this was our common challenge and we had each other. I still remember how some of my teammates supported me in one problem where I was stuck and didn't know how to proceed. Also, we were there for each other, even to support each other in personal areas. It was this feeling of reassurance that I could count on my teammates for everything—in work or even in something personal.

Sheela: So you are saying that you all felt that it was your common challenge or common goal. Is it right to say that you had owned up the goal and made it yours?

Sanjay: Yes, there was a sense of ownership.

Sheela: Now, coming back to the current situation, how do we create an atmosphere where all individuals in the team feel that sense of ownership with the project goals or tasks at hand.

Sanjay: In addition, we also need to think how each one in the team can not only get technical help from others but also feel a sense of comfort and safety in each other's presence.

Sheela: Yes, that's an important point Sanjay. This kind of psychological safety created for employees at the workplace will go a long way in ensuring that the immediate team and the organization play a significant role in ensuring the overall well-being of employees. It is also important to note that this idea of well-being is not restricted to the office premises alone. This is what we carry home too.

Sanjay: In fact, in my experience whenever things are fine at work, my time at home is also very relaxing and I am able to enjoy my time at home. Of course, that's not the case always.

Sheela: True, all of us would have similar experiences. I think this is what the CEO of Amazon, Jeff Bezos, was referring to when he discussed the subject of work–life harmony.

Values Reflection

Introspect and deliberate upon these questions as you go forward in strengthening your organization's culture of values:

- From your point of view, what are the causes of stress at the workplace? Classify them into the following categories: individual (personal), individual (organizational), family life, immediate team, supervisor/manager, organization (culture, systems and policies).
- Of the list of causes of stress, which are the ones that you feel can be mitigated by values? Also specify the values against each cause of stress.
- Do you have the conviction that a values-based atmosphere at workplace can reduce stress levels?
- Think of some situations at workplace where you have seen that values were effective in de-stressing the environment.
- Based on your experience in the organization, what are the three values that every employee in your organization should live by and why?

* * *

शान्तितुल्यं तपो नास्ति न सन्तोषात्परं सुखम् ।
न तृष्णायाः परो व्याधिः न च धर्मो दयापरः ॥

There is no austerity greater than peace; there is no happiness greater than contentment; there is no disease greater than greed; and there is not dharma greater than compassion.

—Subhaashitam

7 Chapter

EMBRACING DIVERSITY

When you focus on someone's disability you'll overlook their abilities, beauty and uniqueness. Once you learn to accept and love them for who they are, you subconsciously learn to love yourself unconditionally.

—Yvonne Pierre

While gender diversity is a very important issue today, be it in the case of politics or in the case of business organizations or other institutions, much of this chapter addresses another crucial matter.

In recent years, technology has made enormous progress to support individuals with disabilities. As shared by Dr Chieko Asakawa (an inventor and IBM fellow who has been blind since the age of 14) in her TED talk, technology has helped her in navigating the path without assistance, recognizing people and their expressions and so on. Of course, some of these are still in developmental stages. She referred to her area of research as 'cognitive assistance'.

As we recognize the fact that humankind is making technological advancements in the area of supporting and assisting persons with disabilities, there is another important aspect here that we need to pay attention to.

However, the more important question is: Do we, as humans, understand the needs of persons with disabilities (either physical or mental) and conduct ourselves accordingly?

In this chapter, we attempt to address this very issue: having employees at the workplace with physical challenges and neurological conditions, how do we conduct ourselves so that we are not only able to make them feel part of the organization but also make the interactions effective in the context of the organization? Remember we are attempting to address only those aspects that are relevant in the context of the organization.

Our own experience of interacting with organizations known for embracing diversity suggests that embracing diversity is not only a higher ideal but leads to enhanced success. Employees feel a sense of pride working at such organizations and their families also exhibit that pride.

Challenges Faced by Persons with Disabilities

Mahesh is an accounts executive with a manufacturing company. He is quite skilled in his job and is as good as, if not better than, his colleagues. It has been two years since joining the company. Things were quite good when he had just joined. But he had a different boss then. She was a very accommodating and understanding lady, although strict and efficient. But the last year had been very challenging. He is part of a new team now. He also has a new boss. Mahesh feels that he has been dumped with very dull tasks. Some of his teammates also ignore him. More often than not, he is depressed, often contemplating quitting this job.

You might think that this has happened to you a few times. But Mahesh's case is different. He has a serious physical disability and he is bound to a wheelchair.

Over the years, some organizations have recruited individuals with physical disabilities for some of the tasks. Needless to say, organizations have begun to recognize this as a solution to their resource pool issues. In the recent past, organizations are also seeing this as a corporate social responsibility.

Often, the biases—both subconscious and conscious—prevent us from seeing the talent in these individuals with disabilities.

Times Are Changing

Just a few years ago, individuals with certain neurological conditions could never hope to have a normal life pursuing a profession or have an opportunity to work, putting their skills towards pursuing the goals of a business organization. Even though people with neurological conditions such as autism, spectrum disorder and dyslexia have extraordinary skills, their potential was going unnoticed, let alone being unutilized.

That scenario is fast-changing!

Organizations are recognizing that individuals with such conditions have extraordinary skills in pattern recognition, memory, mathematics, etc. Companies like SAP, HP, Microsoft, Ford and Ernst & Young have already modified their organizations' processes in order to tap in to the talent pool of individuals with neurological conditions.

Organizations have so far focused primarily on autistic people. It is believed that organizations will also extend this to individuals with other neurological conditions.

Neurodiversity has emerged as a new concept, where diverse neurological conditions are understood to be the result of normal variations in the human genome and hence such differences should be recognized and respected as a social category on par with gender, ethnicity, sexual orientation or disability status.

In their article 'Neurodiversity as a Competitive Advantage', Austin and Pisano (2017) say, 'Perhaps the most surprising benefit is that managers have begun thinking more deeply about leveraging the talents of all employees through greater sensitivity to individual needs'.

They further go on to add: 'Everyone is to some extent differently abled (an expression favored by many neurodiverse people), because we are all born different and raised differently. Our ways of thinking result from both our inherent "machinery" and the experiences that have "programmed" us'.

Situation in India

Seventy per cent of the staff in 20 KFC outlets (in India) are speech and hearing impaired. Close to 80 per cent of the staff at Lemon Tree's newly opened property in Sector 60, Gurugram, India, are people with disabilities. There is growing acceptance of recruiting persons with disabilities across varying kinds of organizations.

Organizations are no longer seeing this as just a CSR initiative but have accepted it as talent pool augmenting strategy.

The Persons with Disabilities (Equal Opportunities, Protection of Rights and Full Participation) Act (of the Government of India), 1995, defines disability as:

- Blindness
- Low vision
- Leprosy cured
- Hearing impairment
- Locomotor disability
- Mental retardation
- Mental illness

Each of these points has been further clarified.

The Rights of Persons with Disabilities Act, 2016, of the Government of India lays down the following principles for empowerment of persons with disabilities[1]:

- Respect for inherent dignity, individual autonomy including the freedom to make one's own choices and independence of persons
- Non-discrimination
- Full and effective participation and inclusion in society
- Respect for difference and acceptance of persons with disabilities as part of human diversity and humanity
- Equality of opportunity
- Accessibility

---

[1]This Act gives effect to the United Nations Convention on the Rights of Persons with Disabilities.

- Equality between men and women
- Respect for the evolving capacities of children with disabilities and respect for the right of children with disabilities to preserve their identities

The Census 2011 (India) highlighted that nearly one-third of the total persons with disabilities are working.

- At an all-India level, 36 per cent of the total persons with disabilities are workers. Among the males with disabilities, 47 per cent are working and among the females with disabilities, only 23 per cent are working.
- In rural India, 25 per cent of the females with disabilities are working, while in urban India, the corresponding figure is 16 per cent.

Organizations Are Gearing Up to This Change

The story of the Helen Keller Awards started way back in 1999 as a result of the findings of a survey conducted of the Top 100 Companies of India by the National Centre for Promotion of Employment for Disabled People (NCPEDP). The results showed that the average percentage of employment of people with disabilities was as follows: in the public sector, 0.54 per cent; in the private sector, 0.28 per cent and in the multinationals, 0.05 per cent.

While the situation has improved to some extent in the past decade and a half, we are still not even close to covering half the percentage of persons with disabilities living in the country.

The NCPEDP Helen Keller Awards were instituted to begin a discourse on equal opportunities for persons with disabilities in the area of employment. The awards are given under the following three categories:

- Category A: Role Model Disabled Person
- Category B: Role Model Supporter of Increased Employment Opportunities for Disabled People
- Category C: Role Model Companies/NGOs/Institutions

What Are the Challenges?

Following are some of the issues relating to having employees in the organization who have physical or neurological disabilities:

- The mindset of people at large regarding disabilities needs substantial change. Everyone sees these only as a weakness.
- The awareness about the various kinds of disabilities is grossly missing.
- Often individuals with disabilities will require some special arrangements to address their essential needs.
- Many individuals do not even declare any information regarding their disabilities to the Human Resources department for fear of discrimination.
- Employees with disabilities are often a victim to reluctance and non-adjustment from fellow employees.
- An organization's leadership is not sufficiently educated regarding this area.
- Because the precedence of such cases is rare or non-existent, it becomes convenient for organizations not to venture into this space, considering this a risk.
- Often fellow employees are not educated about how they should conduct themselves to facilitate effective interaction with the differently abled.
- There are no champions for the cause.
- Organizations do not spend sufficient time or pay attention to this idea, with the result that even small hurdles result in aborting the attempt to engage with such employees.
- Bias—unconscious or conscious—is a major hurdle in this regard.
- Public spaces and organizations' buildings are not designed to accommodate individuals with disabilities.

This is just an indicative list of some of the key issues concerning engaging employees with disabilities. It will, of course, depend on the organizational culture and may vary widely across organizations. Another important point is that employing individuals with disabilities is not widely practised; hence, individuals and organizations will have to learn along the way.

Seeking the Help of Values

Organizations often begin with a policy regarding hiring of differently abled individuals. Many of the organizations that have made significant strides have put in place some or many of the following:

- Sessions to sensitize the senior management and also the managers who directly deal with such employees.
- Special arrangement to cater to the special needs of such employees.
- Development plan which outlines how these differently abled employees will rise in the organization, in other words their growth path.
- Training these differently abled employees—some of them may require additional training to bring them up to speed.
- Identify individuals who can be champions for this cause.
- Have systems and processes which specifically address the needs of the differently abled employees.
- Raising the awareness of other employees towards the employees with disabilities, in particular those who interact with them directly or indirectly.

But this would be just the beginning. To a certain extent, it is easy to implement these things—most being one-time activities. It is most crucial that the culture of the organization and the team in particular be an inclusive one.

Based on the study of initiatives across various organizations to include differently abled individuals, we have identified four values that are most crucial in creating a culture of inclusiveness:

- Respect: Such individuals do not expect any pity, but respect. They expect to be respected for what they are and respected for the special abilities they bring to the organization.
- Empathy: While this is a value which is applicable in every context, an empathetic attitude towards persons with disabilities will go a long way in making them an integral part of the team they belong to.

- Flexibility: People with physical challenges or neurological conditions may not have the usual skills which are so talked about—good communication skills, management skills, some commonly accepted social skills, etc. Here is where management has to be highly flexible in their attitude towards such individuals.
- Patience: Particularly in the initial stages after recruitment and induction, when these employees with disabilities start off in their roles, co-employees need to demonstrate patience in many of the cases. This gives these differently abled employees confidence and helps them slowly but surely to settle into their roles.

These values have to be instilled and lived at all levels—from the senior management and the immediate supervisors to the peers and subordinates.

Gender Diversity

Though the term refers to diversity, the focus is on equitable or fair representation of the genders. There is a lot of public discourse on the subject of gender diversity and also organizations have begun to treat this matter seriously. It also figures prominently as part of the core values of most organizations that have identified values as an important coordinate of their culture.

During our discussions, an executive with a training services provider shared the following episode:

Early on in our organization's growth journey in the late 1980s, a mission and value statement was articulated, regularly discussed and referred—both when people were recruited and subsequently during training programmes. Very early on, within the first few years of existence, the head of the largest business unit at that time was accused by a young executive of an improper behaviour. The actions taken were remarkably fast. Overnight, there was an investigation carried out by a team and the senior executive was asked to go within a day. At that point of time, it was not an easy decision from purely a short-term business view. But the senior management team thought it was vital for the organization to adhere to the stated value of respect for all.

It is important for the senior management of any organization to send the right message about its stance on such matters.

But an important aspect of gender diversity rests on equality. What most organizations seem to address are matters that are enforced by regulatory agencies, for example, 'to have x per cent of women representation in boards'.

In such cases, we are reducing values to become a checklist item that needs to be ticked off. Also, such regulatory guidelines are adhered to by organizations for fear of blacklisting or other punitive measures.

This approach cannot instil a culture where both genders are treated as equal and with respect.

The question to ponder over is 'does offering a percentage of positions to women, in board of directors, ensure equality?'

Some Examples

Cognizant in its Code of Ethics document states the following:

> We must treat others with fairness and respect, and value each other's individual contributions. We never discriminate against a person's legally protected characteristics, such as race, colour, religion, gender, gender identity, age, national origin, sexual orientation, marital status, disability status, or veteran status when we make employment decisions including recruiting, hiring, training, promotion, termination, or providing other terms and conditions of employment.

Source: https://www.cognizant.com/codeofethics.pdf (accessed on 9 April 2019)

Hershey's Code of Ethical Conduct:

> Respect and promote diversity: By working for Hershey, we have made a commitment to treating each other

fairly and with respect. This means we must not make any employment-related decisions based upon a person's race, colour, gender, national origin, age, religion, citizenship status, disability, medical condition, sexual orientation, gender identity, veteran status, marital status or any other basis protected by law.

Source: http://phx.corporate-ir.net/External.File?item=UGFyZW 50SUQ9NDUxMHxDaGlsZElEPS0xfFR5cGU9Mw==&t=1 (accessed on 9 April 2019)

Values Dialogues

Sanjay: While we have a policy to address gender diversity and inclusion, a couple of ladies in my team had come up to say that they are not being assigned challenging opportunities. They said that they had raised these issues with the earlier team lead too. How can we become proactive regarding this and create a system where there is equality?

Sheela: You do recognize that this one does not have any quick fixes. So I don't know if I can really address your concern in the short term. At the same time, I believe this is a very important issue that has to be addressed very fundamentally and sincerely.

Sanjay: What do you mean when you say fundamentally and sincerely?

Sheela: Steps like having a percentage of women in certain positions are very superficial ways. It does not address the problem at its roots. When we are talking about gender inclusion, we are talking of creating a culture where men and women are treated as equal. There is a need for a change in the mindset. That's why I said that the change will not happen until and unless organizations address this fundamentally and sincerely. Any other step will merely be cosmetic and merely to complete a checklist.

Sanjay: Does that mean having some targets do not matter at all?

Sheela: I am not saying that. A target can be a starting point, but it cannot continue to remain that way. By having a target, say 10 per cent women in all middle management roles, and achieving that target, the organization thinks, it has achieved the goal of gender inclusion. You and I know that that is far from the truth. I also believe that having a number like that is detrimental in the long run because it does not bring about equality.

Sanjay: What do you mean by the word equality in this context?

Sheela: Quite simple, both genders have equal opportunities for all roles and positions. And that is the only thing that will eventually lead to a situation where the kind of problem you stated will not happen, where women feel discriminated against.

Sanjay: But isn't it a problem that is to be addressed primarily by organizations and particularly by the senior management?

Sheela: Not really. The organization and its senior management have a responsibility to have a vision and have appropriate policies, and above all have a sincere commitment towards bringing about equality. If they see this only as a regulatory issue and that the organization has to fulfil its responsibility of providing a certain number of positions for women, then that will not percolate down the different levels in the organization. They need to be sincere and seriously committed in both letter and spirit.

Sanjay: What can I do as a team lead to play my part?

Sheela: That's a question everyone should ask themselves. Introspect over the following: Do I recognize men and women as equal (in their right to opportunities) in the context of my own team? Do I discriminate between genders when it comes to challenging tasks and projects? If the answer to either of them is a yes, or you even hesitate to understand your position, then you clearly need to examine your position and mindset fundamentally. That's the responsibility of each of the managers at all levels.

Sanjay: I think you have given me a lot to think about. I shall make a sincere attempt. I shall also discuss the same with the head of our business unit to see what we can do in the short term.

Values Reflections

Introspect and deliberate upon these questions, in the context of your organization, as you go forward in strengthening your organization's culture of values:

- In your organization, do you have a policy regarding recruitment and growth of individuals with disabilities? How effective has it been?
- If you have persons with disabilities in your organization or team, how successful has been the attempt? How successful have these employees been?
- What initiatives have been taken by your organization to address the needs of employees with disabilities?
- What challenges have you faced as a team and organization in hiring and retaining employees with disabilities?
- What core values have helped you and your organization in making such differently abled employees an integral part of your team/organization?

* * *

न क्लेशेन विना द्रव्यमर्थहीने कुतः क्रियाः ।
क्रियाहीने कुतो धर्मो धर्महीने कुतः सुखम् ॥

Devoid of pain from disease, where is the question of taking medicine; devoid of goal, where is the question of activity; devoid of activity, where is the question of dharma; and devoid of dharma, where is the question of attaining happiness.

—Skanda Puraanam

8 Chapter

BUSTING THE MYTHS

> *The values by which we are to survive are not rules for just and unjust conduct, but are those deeper illuminations in whose light justice and injustice, good and evil, means and ends are seen in fearful sharpness of outline.*
>
> **—Jacob Bronowski**

Like any other space of human endeavour, values are not free from imagined myths, and these myths have contributed to the cynicism that persists regarding the adoption of values in business organization.

In this chapter, let us address some of these myths and attempt to shed some light on building a more positive outlook regarding values.

If we do not take a rational approach to understanding values and if we do not dispel these myths, we will never be able to benefit from values.

Myth 1: Values are something personal. They are not relevant in a business organization.

The objectives of any organization (business organization or otherwise) are achieved through individual actions and collaboration between individuals. In other words, the individual is the fundamental building block of any organization.

The moment we refer to the term human, qualities, virtues or values are the only thing that make us human. Values are the only thing that has held the society together for centuries now.

Values are the only thing that built the organization. Values are the only thing that has brought the organization to the current position.

Where is the question of delinking the organization from values?

Instead of saying 'values are personal', the right thing is to say 'values are what make us human'. Values and humans cannot be separated in any context.

Myth 2: We already have ethical accounting practices; we don't need values.

We have already discussed this point at length in Chapter 2. Accounting practices ought to be ethical; it cannot be any other way. If accounting practices are not ethical, it violates the law of the land. There is a law enforcement machinery in place to address it, if there is any kind of transgression.

Yes, organizations take up this matter to ensure that there are no violations in this regard. It is also in their best interests because money is involved. Organizations also are concerned that there is no embezzlement of funds or other resources.

But remember, values are not just about good or right accounting practices.

Violation of values is not illegal, but in some contexts it may be considered inhuman. Many of the subtle violations of values may not even be noticed, let alone acted upon. But recognizing the need to strengthen values across the organization pays dividends to the organization and above all creates an environment which individuals like to be part of.

Myth 3: Values are all about right and wrong, and good and bad.

We approach the subject of values not from the point of view of doing good, but from the point of view of doing what is appropriate in the context and what makes the interaction between any two humans effective and productive. One need not see it as doing the right thing or doing good.

Consider the case of a meeting to discuss a strategy to combat the low sales of a flagship product of a company. For this meeting to be successful, the following points are important:

- All concerned are given an opportunity to express themselves without fear (fairness)
- Everyone present is respectful to the views of each one present (respect for others)
- Even if the solution comes from someone who is from the junior rung of the organization, others should have the humility to accept it (humility)
- Even if mistakes had been committed, concerned employees accept their mistakes and do what is necessary to redress the situation, instead of justifying their actions (fairness)
- All concerned place all the relevant facts on the table, so that the situation can be dealt with utmost urgency (transparency)

These values of fairness, respect for others, humility, fairness, transparency, etc., are essential elements in the interactions of all those present in the meeting. It has nothing to do with moral right or moral wrong.

Myth 4: The idea of values is something nice to talk about, not practical.

From the discussion in the context of the previous situation of the meeting, isn't it evident that values are an essential component of every interaction between any two individuals in the organization?

Values are not only practical in every context of the organization but are also an imperative.

Without the values, every interaction, every conversation, every decision and every communication carry no meaning.

Myth 5: Pay-offs from values, if at all, are only in the long term.

The crucial point to note regarding values is that values are already at work in everything that is going on. In other words, we are already reaping the benefits of values.

All we need to do is to become more sensitive to the role of values in all our interactions, and if we are able to strengthen the values, the resultant benefits will be far greater. Values are what sustain relationships between individuals, families, societies and nations.

Myth 6: If we are thinking of values in the organization, then we lack values today.

This is a very incorrect notion. When a team of individuals come together with the idea of forming an organization to achieve a certain objective, they carry with them a certain set of values.

In fact, their coming together is enabled by the values they possess, and that alignment in values and thought process among the individuals facilitates the process of setting up the organization.

In other words, every organization, irrespective of what stage it happens to be in, has a set of values and that verily form the organization's culture.

So when the organization contemplates and starts discussing the subject of values, it has acknowledged the importance of values and has also recognized a need to strengthen the values in order to take the organization forward.

Myth 7: It's not possible to instil values in a business environment.

This is another major misconception—values are either already present or absent, and if they are absent, they cannot be instilled.

Nothing can be farther from the truth. We are just quoting an example to prove this point. Bridgewater Associates chose to include transparency as a principle they wanted to instil in their culture. And this did not happen in one day and without its share of obstacles. But it certainly did happen, and in fact they took transparency to a very high level and became a benchmark for all to emulate.

Like all initiatives, this too begins with a first step. Everything else that follows boils down to perseverance. One of the key foundational values required to embark on this journey of values is perseverance. Organizations find it easy to begin various initiatives. But unless the organization perseveres in the effort, nothing succeeds.

And in this journey there are no shortcuts. One of the common obstacles everyone faces in instilling values is to change the mindset of 'values cannot be instilled'.

* * *

धृतिः क्षमा दमोऽस्तेयं शौचमिन्द्रियनिग्रहः ।
धीर्विद्या सत्यमक्रोधो दशकं धर्मलक्षणम् ॥

Firmness of resolve, patience, self-control, non-stealing, cleanliness, restraint of the sense organs, reflection, learning, truthfulness and freedom from anger are the 10 characteristics of dharma.

—Subhaashitam

9 Chapter

SYMPHONY, NOT AN ORGANIZATION

Living in a way that reflects one's values is not just about what you do, it is also about how you do things.

—Deborah Day

What Are Values-Based Organizations?

A values-based organization is one where:

- The organization has chosen to strive towards values orientation in all aspects of its function and business.
- Employees of the organization strive to uphold values in all their dealings with each other, with customers, vendors, regulators, government agencies and any other external entities dealing with the organization.

For the purpose of implementation, the management may focus on specific values and decide that the collective endeavour will be to ensure that all employees live these values in the context of every facet of the organization's business and function.

Consider the cells in the human body. Even if one cell goes down, it can affect the entire body. 'That is an extreme argument', some might say. In the context of quality policies in organizations, the philosophy of zero defect echoes the previous sentiment.

In today's context of extreme competition in all sectors, do we have a choice regarding product or service quality? Most organizations have undertaken to strive towards the goal of zero defects.

Similarly, in the case of values, an organization may not reach a stage of 100 per cent values orientation. But the organization can certainly strive for it.

That striving is what human civilization is all about!

Benefits of Being Values Based

Values-based organizations are not just about creating an environment where individuals do not commit 'wrong'.

Of course, all benefits are not directly measurable in terms of monetary value as corporations and shareholders are normally accustomed to.

According to an executive from an IT services organization in India, 'Any attempt to measure the benefits in terms of monetary value will entirely defeat the very purpose of such initiatives to make the environment values based'.

The following are some of the benefits of building and nurturing values-based organizations:

- Enhanced productivity and excellence which fuels business growth
- Higher instances of innovation and creativity because the environment is free from inhibiting factors
- Better relationships with customers and hence better customer retention
- More healthy work environment and one with lesser stress[1]
- Better ability to weather challenges of times and able to sustain themselves for long term

An accounts executive, who was in the third year of her career, with a BPO organization, had the following experience:

---

[1]Studies have shown that stress-free environments lead to greater productivity and quality.

We had bagged a new and important project, and I was chosen as one of the three members to execute the first phase of this project. We were to travel overseas in about a week's time. When we had just three more days for travel, my father fell ill. He needed care and attention, and my support was critical. I requested that I be allowed to stay back and someone else travel in my place for the project. The head of the business unit was quite upset and said that that was not an option. However, my immediate boss, the project manager, came to my rescue. He supported my decision and explicitly told me that he will back my decision, and the business head was not very happy about the project manager's stance. My boss found a replacement and made the necessary arrangements.

It was a great lesson learnt for me to stand by the people you work with, and an example of teamwork I cherish till today, even after having completed 20 years working in a few business organizations.

From the individual's point of view, being values based results in the following benefits:

- Unassailable strength
- Unshakeable conviction
- Clarity of thought
- Unambiguous decision-making
- Stress-free personality

Corporate Social Responsibility

The benefits of being a values-based organization go beyond the current generations of individuals who comprise the institution.

Since the employees spend most of their wakeful hours in the context and confines of the organization, the organization's culture has the potential of making a deep impact on the values orientation of the individuals.

If you know of families where if even one of the parents is associated with the armed forces (army, navy, air force), you will find that often the children begin to embody the values espoused by the parents, which reflect the armed forces background.

This is a natural process of osmosis which the employees go through in a values-based organization. Over time, the values of the organization become an integral part of the individual's personality.

In fact, when organizations or recruitment agencies come across a candidate from a particular organization, and they take interest in that candidate, it is primarily for the values they espouse from that culture. In such cases, it is not just the skills that the organization is interested in, but the values.

Values-based organizations nurture and are nurtured by values-based individuals.

Such individuals will influence the creation and nurturing of values-based families. Often it is seen that values-based families create a sound bedrock for nurturing values-based children. And these children form the backbone of values-based society of the future.

So a values-based organization over the years contributes to building a values-based society.

This is true corporate social responsibility!

The vision of such organizations goes beyond the commonly understood notion of service and social responsibility. It redefines the purpose of the corporation by its very existence and contribution to the society. It has far-reaching impact on the organization, employees, families of employees, society, nation and the globe.

Values-Based Organization is Each Individual's Responsibility

Let us look at the family, a unit we all identify with. The well-being of the family and relationships among the family members are based on values. This means, each individual member of the family shares a conviction in those values and all the members collectively live those values.

Even if one member of the family deviates from the values, we will not feel that way about the entire family. Most, if not all, would have experienced that the family based on values is often a more peaceful and happy family.

When we recognize this in the context of a family consisting of merely a handful of members, what then to speak of the business organization which has so many more members and that too coming from diverse backgrounds!

Why is it important?

The organization has to function as an integrated unit for it to meet its purpose. When we say 'integrated', we are referring to the individual members of the organization (i.e., the employees), functioning in harmony, like the cells of the living body. This harmony results when each member of the organization is values based and also understands the purpose of the business and what his/her role is in the overall plan. In integrity of each individual lies the integrity of the organizational entity.

> *Being values-based is not an option;*
> *it is a responsibility; it has to be a compulsion.*

Does Having a Statement of Values and Principles Serve the Purpose?

The management of the organization may feel that it has very stringent and vigilant audits and hence the organization is free from fraud. It is under a great delusion. It has also become corporate culture to be concerned about only those parameters that can be measured; therefore, organizations monitor systems which directly relate to accounts and finance. Let us recall what Albert Einstein said, 'Not everything that can be counted counts, and not everything that counts can be counted'.

We often hear organizations claim: 'we have a quality policy, and a robust set of systems, processes and procedures'. Does this ensure quality? The organization may even have been certified against some quality standards. Does that ensure quality? Certainly not!

Similar is the case in the context of values, ethics, Code of Conduct, principles, etc.

What are some of the challenges faced by organizations in living values?

Let us examine a particular scenario in an organization which is engaged in providing high-end products and services in the Telecom Sector.

One of the codes in the organization's Code of Conduct stated the following: 'An employee shall neither receive nor offer or make, directly or indirectly, any illegal payments, remuneration, gifts, donations or comparable benefits that are intended, or perceived, to obtain uncompetitive favours for the conduct of the organization's business'.

An employee X has been trying to close a deal with a customer for products and services which totals to a substantial amount, which is significant percentage of X's annual target. With not much time left for the year ending, X is under a lot of pressure to close this deal. There are no other prospects in his pipeline. So if he doesn't close this deal, he will fall well short of his target, which might engender a drastic measure on the part of his management.

X discovers through some of his contacts at the customer organization that if a small percentage of the deal value is offered as a kickback to a senior executive Y in the customer organization, the deal will be guaranteed.

The following questions arise:

- Even though the organization has a Code of Conduct, do the employees recall the principles when the situation requires them to do so?

- Even if the employee recalls that there is a Code of Conduct, does he/she know unambiguously how the situation at hand has to be dealt with as per the stated Code of Conduct?
- It is possible that the Code of Conduct does not explicitly address the situation at hand, but it is possible that the action may be an in-principle violation of the core values of the organization. Are the employees trained and empowered to act accordingly?
- Even if they remember the Code of Conduct, does the organization's culture sufficiently inspire/empower the employees to not fall to the temptation?
- Has the senior management of the organization created an atmosphere which enables the employees to feel confident that they should uphold the core values of the organization, even if it results in loss of an opportunity (in the case of losing the contract)?
- Even if the organization's culture gives enough indications of what the core values of the organization are, does the employee (X in this case) have enough moral courage and fortitude to adhere to the organization's codes?
- If the employee X falls for the temptation, resulting in violation of the Code of Conduct, but bags this huge business contract, how does the organization respond to the violation?
- If the employee X does not fall for the temptation and upholds the Code of Conduct of the organization, but has lost the contract, what is the organization's response towards X?

The situation and the various questions X faces in this context are very subtle and cannot be enforced. As far as the employee is concerned, there is threat of consequences which puts enormous pressure on X to act in a certain manner.

Can a mere policy statement or a Code of Conduct document decide how X will act? Certainly not.

Analysis of Values: Some Examples

Since the genesis, definition, adoption and finally pervasiveness of the values are closely tied to the culture of the organization, values become somewhat personal to the particular organization.

To address the same situation, two different organizations—of the same size, industry, etc.—may come up with two entirely different sets of values. And the language, the description, the presentation, the communication, etc., of those values will depend on the organization's culture. Because of that, it is difficult and perhaps does not make much sense in commenting upon a set of values of an organization, if one is not part of the organization's culture.

However, here we take up the analysis of some values, so that we are able to understand the different facets of the definition of values. This will help identify values for your organization, and if already identified, it will help in clarifying the definition of the values, and in communication of the values to all across the organization.

Note: The values presented in the following examples are not fictional. They are the ones certain organizations have adopted and we have picked them up from their respective websites.

Value: Customer Focus

Organization: Jet Airways

Many organizations identify customer focus, customer centricity, customer obsession, customer success, etc., as one of their core values. Following are some points we would like you to introspect over:

- Every organization has a customer; in other words, without a customer, there is no business. What are we saying by stressing on customer focus?
- What about the customer is the focus?
- How does this value apply to a software programmer who is developing software to manage the company's payroll?

- Have you applied the what-enables-it analysis to this value? What does it lead us to?
- What about the vendors of the organization?
- Does this mean employee is not the focus?

Value: Teamwork

Organization: Alibaba Group

Organizations, without exception, are made of individuals and teams. So can any organization survive without teamwork? Examine the following points in the context of having teamwork as one of the core values of the organization:

- What does it mean to have teamwork as a value? What does it mean?
- How will you articulate this point to all the employees of the organization?
- How will you guide employees in practising this value?
- How will you demonstrate this value? When you talk about demonstrating teamwork, you are actually high-lighting aspects such as openness, listening, transparency, accepting all points of view and so on. So what does it mean to just say 'teamwork is a core value'? Is it core? Or is it what results when certain chemistry happens between the individuals in the team?
- It is more important to examine that makes teamwork happen, or what makes teamwork effective and excellent.

Value: Proactive Involvement

Always look for ways to add value in everything we do by going the extra mile.

Organization: Apollo Hospitals

Organizations need to take sufficient care in identifying and phrasing the values. While the intent behind this one might have been noble, this seems like a vague, feel-good platitude. Following are some points to ponder over in this case:

- Are values about making feel-good statements or motherhood statements?
- The vagueness in this statement is quite prominent. While making such a statement in a particular context, it may not be vague. But when you make it a general statement to all, what do you think will be the interpretation made by different employees?
- How is anyone supposed to practise it?
- How will you know when someone has violated this value?
- While this might appear to be an inspiring statement as part of some instruction or speech, how will you know that you have achieved it?
- Does it have more than a feel-good value?

Value: Safety

Organization: Singapore Airlines

Examine this core value from the point of view of the definition we have adopted in this book. From the viewpoint of the airlines and its customers, this is a very crucial parameter. Introspect the following points:

- Safety is a performance parameter and very fundamental to the entire business. When we talk of values, we are referring to the quality or trait of the human; in other words, it's a human attribute.
- In the same manner, 'on time every time' is an important service level agreement for the flights, but it does not become a core value.
- Does this apply to all stakeholders of the organization?
- The important question to ask is, 'what qualities should all the employees espouse' so that it forms the foundation for the business.

Challenges Faced by Employees

While both the organization and the individual benefit from values, this path is certainly not a bed of roses. Executives at different levels of the organization have shared the following issues with regard to their stance in the sphere of values:

- Many employees feel that values are beyond the sphere of their influence.
- There are those in the organization in positions of responsibility who offer only lip service to the subject of values; there is a big gap between the talk and the walk.
- Others are not able to see the need to act in a values-oriented manner and they feel that this whole area relating to values is unnecessary in the context of the workplace.
- Those who have violated values have done better in the organization in terms of position, compensation, recognition, etc.
- Those who have violated codes of values have got away with their violations.
- One has been ridiculed and mocked for taking a values-based stance.
- Not able to demonstrate any objective reason to the non-believers, as to why values are critical to the workplace.
- There are too many cynics in the system. As a result, the cause for values is drowned.
- Over a period of time, the various challenges relating to values (caused by some or many of the aforementioned situations) have caused a lot of stress to oneself, which has also taken its toll on physical health.

Perseverance Is the Key

A strong culture of values can alone address such conflicts in the workplace and make it convenient for employees to take the appropriate decisions and also uphold the values and principles identified in the organization. The following are very crucial:

- Demonstration of values by senior management in situations of such conflicts.
- Role models who have made it a habit to live by the values and codes of the organization.
- There are no negative consequences of upholding values, particularly when there is a negative business impact.

- Managers/supervisors stand by the employees in their decisions in upholding values.
- There is clarity in the definition and interpretation of values across the entire organization.
- For the culture of values to become an organization-wide phenomenon, and for it to be sustained over time, perseverance is the key.

Remember the following:

- You are not accountable or responsible for values of others.
- You can only express yourself, you can't force values on others.
- Organizations can take punitive action for violations of Code of Conduct, but they can't do anything to ensure 100 per cent adherence to values-based interactions.

What Is Values Violation?

The word fraud is generally used in the context of any transgression in organizations. However, fraud is defined as 'deliberate deception, trickery or cheating intended to gain an advantage', 'an act or instance of such deception'. Some may find the term fraud very strong or harsh. Do we really want to use a term like fraud? It seems so gross and strong. More importantly, it misses out on the subtler transgressions which go unnoticed.

Keeping this in mind, let us use the term values violation. As we shall see later, this is a more fundamental term and takes into account anything that is a deviation from values-oriented conduct/behaviour. You may also consider a term like values transgression.

We define values violation as any infringement or violation with regard to values.

From the point of view of the focus of this book, we can broadly classify the violations into three categories:

- Grossly unlawful
- Gross
- Subtle

The classification is more to understand the violations, their causes and also to be able to find solutions to address them.

We can examine the different values violations based on their characteristics which are as follows:

- Not visible, not apparent but is there under the surface
- Is there and everyone knows it but chooses to ignore
- Very evident; everyone has accepted it as a practice
- Very evident; no one says anything
- You are ignorant to the fact that it is a violation

Grossly Unlawful Values Violations

These are the ones which are very apparent and can be very clearly articulated, and for which the organization can clearly have some Code of Conduct. These are very gross in nature, in that they are very obvious and can be proved. These are typically termed as fraud and are also unlawful. People often associate only accounts and finance to be domains for values violations, but there are many others which fall in this category.

Following are some examples:

- Intellectual property violations: Individuals copy data/information from the Internet as well as other sources and present the same as their work. In the area of IT services, employees tend to copy software design and programmes from past projects and reuse them violating intellectual property rights.
- Accounting and billing transgressions: Cooking up account books to present organization's accounts favourably or to show inflated revenues.
- Graft: Depending on the nature of the business, the acquisition of business or revenue through unfair or illegal means.
- Personal accounting: Artificial reimbursement claims, wrong entries in travel claims, fake bills, etc., are quite common.
- Using office resources for personal use: There are also instances when employees are seen using office space

for moonlighting. Individual also use office hours to run parallel jobs outside the purview of the organization. Of course, there are some organizations which are liberal in these contexts and we are not referring to them here.

- Interpersonal interactions: Bias on account of gender, race, community, religious difference, etc., is also a serious violation; trend of using abusive language or profanity during interactions.

Gross Values Violations

These violations can also be discerned easily and disrupt the effective functioning in the organization. Since the word unlawful is missing, it does not mean that these are lawful. These violations have a negative impact on the health and well-being of the organization and bring down the morale of the employees. There is a thin line dividing gross unlawful and gross values violations.

Following are some examples:

- Human Resource management: Favouritism and lack of transparency in hiring, project allocations, performance appraisals, promotions, lay-offs, etc.
- Lack of transparency in decision-making: This can cause great damage, both in the short term and long term. Some may feel that there is a thin line between poor execution or inability and values violation here. Values-based organizations will be able to draw clear distinction between the two.
- Project proposals, business plans and bids: The pressure to meet targets and procure business often leads to drafting of proposals and business plans that become very fictional rather than being factual.
- Manipulating social media campaigns: Platforms such as Facebook, Instagram, Twitter, etc., are being used to artificially enhance popularity and also send out fictitious public opinion.

- Offering lip service: Perhaps one of the greatest contri-
butors to employee dissatisfaction is not walking the talk.
Management tends to make promises and commitments
when faced with situations, which are not subsequently
followed up.
- Vision violations: It is when the management transgresses
the vision statement of the organization in letter and
spirit. The founders while envisioning the culture and future
of the organization adopt certain values which are explicitly
stated. Any violations of this kind are very fundamental
and have far-reaching impact on the very identity of the
institution.

Subtle Values Violations

In contrast to the gross violations, subtle values violations by
employees are hard to discern, except perhaps by people who
are working closely with them. Sometimes, you may find that
these are not even transgressions of stated values, but in the
context of the situation at hand, it is a violation. Often these
violations are first felt within the team, and in some cases may
spread to other teams in the organization.

Following are some examples:

- Non-conformance: Non-conformance to stated processes
and guidelines is a very common violation, at times not
easy to detect. Sometimes there could be compliance as
per letter, but it could be a violation in spirit.
- Wastage of resources: Wastage of any kind of resources
or being lavish in spending is again something that is not
technically a violation but in the long run may impact the
organizational culture and performance.
- Lack of empathy or compassion: Not being empathetic
towards others is something that gradually or often surely
erodes the trust of employees towards the establishment.
In certain situations, it is even difficult to establish that
there has been a violation of the values of empathy and

compassion, because these are very subtle qualities of the human mind.

- Lack of respect towards individuals: This too is a very subtle matter, and at times people's opinion may differ regarding the violation. However, repeated violations impacts the morale and performance of the individual(s) concerned, and also soon negatively impacts the others around.
- Lack of commitment to work or lack of industry: Not putting the required effort to complete the job assigned. This is difficult to comprehend but soon establishes a culture of mediocrity in the team or organization. Here, it is not difficult for a manager to draw a distinction between lack of commitment/ownership and inability.
- Taking credit for someone else's work: This is also an often shared problem at work place and comes in various forms and dimensions.
- No feedback from the employees: Employees do not give feedback to the organization at the right time, which can often help in setting right issues before they blow up and become impossible to deal with.
- Tardiness: Arriving late for work and meetings, not keeping appointments, missing deadlines in projects, etc.

There are areas where people are not aware that there is a values violation. In certain organization's cultures, some violations have become so prevalent that they are no longer seen as violations. They have almost become standard operating procedures. This is not uncommon. Unless we recognize these areas and correct them, violations can spread in other areas as well. The more it remains unnoticed or ignored, the stronger the violation begins to grow.

Following are some examples of such violations:

- Violations in process implementation
- Misuse of office resources
- Delay in start of meetings
- Casual/abusive language
- False claims (accounting)

Instances of Violations at Team Meetings

We can see team meetings as a microcosm of the organization's culture. Herein we are able to see values in action. At the same time, any values violations here are indicators or red flags for management to take note of and prevent these from spreading. Here are some reported violations:

- Members do not follow a collaborative approach in arriving at decisions. Some senior members tend to dominate decision-making and not everyone gets to voice their views.
- Minutes of meeting do not reflect the actual proceedings. Sometimes minutes are prepared while no meetings were held. Not informing everyone uniformly about the agenda of the meeting thereby not allowing all to be equally prepared for the meeting.
- Phone calls and texting go on while meeting is in progress.
- There is no transparency while taking decisions.
- Abusive language is used often, people are admonished unpleasantly in public, bad-mouthing someone who is not in the meeting.
- Meetings do not start or end on time, participants walk in at different times into the meeting, not being prepared for meetings.

Stages in the Causes of Values Violations

Based on our surveys, it appears that the individuals fall into the trap gradually. Figure 9.1 shows some of the stages of influence the individual goes through in being driven to a violation. It is not suggested that there is a hierarchy here. It helps us understand the behaviour pattern so that appropriate interventions can be thought of.

Figure 9.1 Stages of Causes of Violations

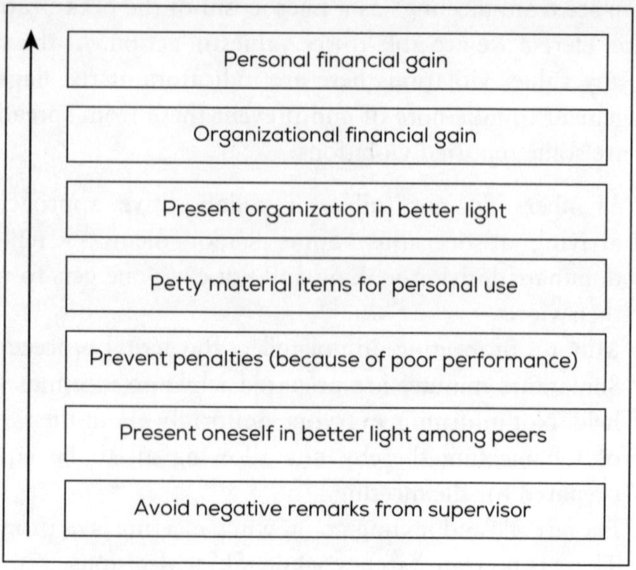

Personal financial gain

Organizational financial gain

Present organization in better light

Petty material items for personal use

Prevent penalties (because of poor performance)

Present oneself in better light among peers

Avoid negative remarks from supervisor

Impact of Values Violations

Impact on the Work Environment and Culture

Repeated values violations begins to show upon the daily work culture in the organization. In the long run, it threatens the very survival of the organization. Following are some of the common problems shared with us:

- Violations are the new normal
- Stressful, insecure work environment
- (Any) Communication viewed suspiciously
- Problems hidden rather than solved till they lead to a crisis
- Rumour mongering, gossiping, backbiting and employee attrition
- Lack of teamwork
- Poor organizational performance

Following is an interesting anecdote shared by a senior project manager of an IT services organization in India. While the violation of values occurred outside the context of the organization, still it could have had a very serious impact on the organization.

As an organization that was committed to quality as an important attribute of whatever we do in the organization, we had established systems and processes for every aspect of our functioning. These processes were being audited periodically for adherence to various standards and frameworks. On this occasion, we were about to embark on an ISO audit. On the first day of this audit, I was given the responsibility, along with another colleague, of picking up the auditor, who had just flown in from the USA a couple of days ago. We left the hotel in my car and I was at the steering wheel. Having not been very familiar with that area, I took a wrong turn into a one-way street. I hadn't seen any 'no entry' sign there. And soon enough a cop waved at me to stop. I stopped and stepped out of the car to go to the spot where he stood. I tried to explain that I couldn't see any 'no entry' sign there. But he wouldn't budge. I was also getting anxious—I had a guest from overseas, who was being driven to the office to audit us, and above all we had very little time before the kick-off meeting in the office. By this time, I was sweating. And what impression would our overseas guest have? These and other such thoughts were pouring in. In a sudden impulsive action, I took out a currency note and handed it over to him. He handed me back my driving licence. And as I stepped into the car, our guest, the auditor said, 'So you bribed him'. I was not sure if it was a question or a statement. I just said, 'yes'.

This is one episode in my corporate career that I most regret. More importantly, at that juncture, I had become a poor representative of the organization. I was taking the organization down with me. The next day, we did have our ISO certification renewed, but it was a very strong lesson that I learnt that day. It seemed like an innocuous act, but through that I could have ruined the reputation of the organization in a serious manner.

The lesson for me was any act, however harmless, could potentially harm the reputation of the organization irreversibly. It is not just an act performed by me for which I am responsible for; it could harm the others around and the entire organization and the business.

Here is a point you can ponder over: If you were in the position of the auditor, what impression would you draw about the organization? Would this episode have coloured your assessment of the organization?

Impact on the Employees

Let us begin this discussion by presenting what a fresher in a major Telecom company shared with us:

That year (a year after my joining as a fresher) the company did very well; profits soared. While the company had been talking about a substantial raise for the employees in the next year's revision, there was not such raise. I as a fresher was deeply disappointed. I had built up my expectations and had even planned to purchase a motorbike.

That action of the management, and my disappointment, left a very lasting negative impression. It struck at the very root of my value system. However, when I look back I do feel that there could have been a very open communication from the management explaining their action and could have addressed the grievances of many in the organization, who were not only expecting that raise but also were dependent on it.

As illustrated by this instance, violations have a deep impact on employees. Sometimes individuals carry their impressions across organization's boundaries. Following are some ways employees are impacted as a result of repeated violations:

- Creates a lack of trust amongst employees and also in management
- Blurs the boundaries between what is a violation and what is values-oriented conduct

- Encourages individuals to take care of their own interest rather than the organization, customer and others
- Promotes mediocrity, insensitivity, indifference and cynicism
- Diminishes joy, commitment and inspiration at work and can even lead to split among teams
- Makes the individual insecure, weak and confused
- Creates an atmosphere of fear of making mistakes, resulting in loss of productivity, innovation, risk-taking ability and creativity
- Leads to staff becoming cynical or disgruntled—eventually leaving the organization
- Adversely shaping their thinking for the rest of their career (especially in the case of young individuals)

Why Do Violations Take Place?

Muel Kaptein (2012) in 'Why Good People Sometimes Do Bad Things? 52 Reflections on Ethics at Work' has identified the various possible factors that cause values violations. Our own discussions with employees and managers revealed the following reasons for values violations:

- Pressure to meet business targets (realistic or unrealistic), time pressures to meet deadlines, low on resources to perform the assigned projects/tasks
- Lack of management commitment: Management of the organization is not committed to values; they offer lip service; they violate values on different occasions. Their conduct seems to convey that they are beyond values, while others have to be values oriented. Management is seen violating values and that sends wrong signals.
- Unrealistic targets: These could be relating to revenue, profits, project milestones, individual performance, etc.
- Always and relentlessly driven by bottom line: Everything is about the bottom line and there is no other inspiring or motivating factor.
- Stress to retain one's position in the team, organization, in a location, in a department, etc., or impending threat of a lay-off

- Fear of adverse performance evaluation, fear of being reprimanded
- Lack of transparency: Discouraging feedback, not acting on feedback sought
- Absence of clear communications regarding commitment to values
- Autocratic style of the manager/supervisor and/or senior management leading to employees feeling disrespected

What are the thoughts behind the values violations? Here are some responses shared (verbatim) by people on why they were part of values violation(s) or why they did not prevent someone else committing a violation:

- Have seen others do it and also get away with it.
- Everyone does it.
- It is a very small thing. I am still a very honest person.
- I am in control. I am doing this with complete awareness.
- By doing this or saying this, I am not hurting anyone.
- Nobody is going to notice this small piece of 'not-so-perfect' work in the context of the full project.
- Many are doing it right; so my wrong will not get noticed; or will not affect the overall project.
- Nobody is there to see me jump the red light.
- I am in a hurry. I am sure someone else will help.
- I don't want to come across as a difficult person.
- This is the culture here.
- Why get into trouble needlessly.
- Obviously the seniors here know—there is no point in getting into this.

Recovering from Violations

Values violations do occur, whatever may be the cause. However, the recovery from these violations also speaks volumes of the management culture.

Let us examine the following experiences shared by an HR Manager with a manufacturing company:

In our organization, values were articulated and taken seriously. Lapses in values were dealt with an appropriate and timely manner. Episode 1: There was a lapse in integrity in an instance of billing. The senior executive was asked to leave the very day it was detected. Episode 2: There was an incident where a manager called a subordinate, who was on leave for some time on account of severe ill health and spoke harshly to her. When this was brought to the notice of HR, swift action was taken. The manager's team was disbanded and he was asked to take a non-people management role till he developed the skills and mindset of leading people.

These episodes clearly showed that one can be empathetic and strict at the same time, a very important combination in life, not only at the workplace but also in all spheres of life. Just because we are loving and kind to a child does not mean that we cannot be strict with a child.

While there was zero tolerance to values violations, the culture of empathy provided an opportunity to correct oneself.

This ability of the organization culture goes a long way in creating a respect for values-oriented behaviour.

To conclude this discussion on violations:

The typical question that comes up is 'Are these important from the organization's point of view?' Nobody stops to think that speaking abusively or wastage is a violation. Examine the following:

It is not that one has to convert violations into money to be able to assess their importance. Not all damages are money related. What manifests as minor violations starts growing; these minor ones start becoming more widespread and it is just a matter of time before the violations start becoming more and more serious.

Non–values-based organizations are like an unhealthy body. Initially, you may ignore some minor ailments, but we have seen that often they become serious.

Why do we need to delve into the subject of values violations in such detail? This tells those concerned what damage the violations cause to the organizational culture and the ability of the organization to perform to its potential. A careful analysis will give the organization clues as to what needs to be done to not only prevent further damage but also to take the organization towards its intended goals.

We cannot stand values violations;
how then can we indulge in them?

Values in Multinational Organizations

Depending on the size of the organization, a critical number of the senior leadership has to be committed to values. Wherever you don't see any gap in walking the talk by the leadership, rest of the organization will not deviate from the path of values. The moment there is a dilution, rest of the organization too will soon follow. Recovering from a fall is a great challenge, much more challenging than building it from scratch.

In the case of a multinational organization, an organization that is spread across different geographies and cultures, the complexity involved in the context of building a culture of values is further enhanced.

This is what the COO of a newly established entity in India said:

> Our organization was set up almost a decade ago in the US and has an established Code of Conduct. Now the global CEO is trying to push the same culture and the Code of Conduct (which exists in the headquarters in the US), into the new set up in India. There is some resistance from the team here. The culture there was created gradually over a period of time. The global management expects all that will get instilled here immediately. Their point is that it is all cooked and ready; there should be no problem.

There is an important point that comes out from this experience. It is not very practical to expect that what is 'cooked and ready' can easily be implemented in another country just like that. When it comes to matters relating to the organization culture, it is related to the human dimension, and that will depend on the local prevailing culture and customs.

For example, in some cultures, it may not be so easy to achieve transparency or openness. This is primarily because as people they may be reticent and private when it comes to various matters at the workplace.

Another young executive who had recently joined a relatively small company in India, which is a subsidiary of a large global IT services company, had the following to say: 'Somehow the global management team thinks that sitting somewhere in Europe, you can pass on the organization values document and remotely control the creation of a values culture in India, without getting to understand our life and problems here'. We had asked in response, 'Are the employees in India rejecting the values because they did not originate here?' Her response was, 'That was not the initial response. There were some difficulties early in the implementation; then there was some pressure to push through quickly. Then people began to resist'.

While the subject of values in the context of multicultural organizations is a vast subject by itself, we present a few points for due consideration:

- Matters relating to culture even in the context of business organizations will vary widely when we move across geographical boundaries. In the case of a country like India, this change is very palpable even when we move from a northern state to a southern state.
- There is a need to understand local cultures, customs and societal behaviours while planning anything in the context of organization culture, including values.
- It is true that the basic human values like integrity, honesty, openness, fairness, kindness, empathy, compassion, etc., remain the same across geographies. But how these values manifest at the behavioural and interactional level, there will be subtle changes.

- The management of the organization needs to be sensitive to the local culture and customs and be respectful of the same.

'Values Health' of an Organization

What are the indicators of the health in the context of the values culture of an organization? This has to be viewed from everyone's perspective, that is, from the viewpoint of all the different stakeholders of the organization.

Following are some of the pointers to be sensitive to:

- Are employees on the frontlines, either dealing with customers or vendors, empowered to act the right way based on the principles of the organization, without having to check through a series of seniors in the organization?
- Do employees have fun at the workplace? From an employee's perspective, if he/she has to drag oneself to work every day, it says something about the environment. This is not just a function of the work content but an indicator of the culture of the organization.
- Are the organization's values upheld because that is the commitment and not because of the wish to be seen as being values based?
- Does the organization respect and adhere to various commitments like gender inclusion, because they believe in the value, and not because violation of it will lead to being blacklisted by a regulatory agency?
- Is adhering to values being driven by compliance against a checklist and not by living those values in spirit?
- Is the talk and walk consistent? Suppose, as an organization you have chosen 'health and well-being of employees' as one of the core values. In one of the meetings, a member of the senior management team said that 'employees need to take care of their health, otherwise it increases the cost to company'. Such statements do not convey the commitment of the organization to values.

- Does values adherence depend on a particular role, position or power? When you talk of a value, say integrity, it is important to act with integrity whether it is in the context of employee, vendor, customer or a government agency the organization interacts with. The value upheld is independent of who you are interacting with. If empathy is a value we have chosen, then we have to be empathetic to all irrespective of the seniority, designation, etc.

- Do managers across the organization, at all levels, conduct themselves on stated values in terms of how they tackle problems, how they act when in crisis, how they take decisions, how they drive performance?

- How forthcoming employees are providing feedback, especially on instances of dilution of values?

- How swiftly the organization addresses values violations and prevents repeated occurrences are very fundamental qualities required for building a stable values culture. Cumulative effect of small instances of violations is what leaves an impression on the individual to say, 'We don't have a culture of values'.

- How seamless is the collaboration among members of teams?

- Is there tolerance for regular and petty violations? Following is what an administration manager of a public sector company shared:

Some years back, we had just then bought our first laser printer. We found that people were constantly walking away with A4 sheets that they would take home. We didn't do anything, thinking it is after all a few sheets of paper. But this habit of walking away with just paper soon included other office supplies and quarterly bill for office supplies went through the roof. Had we addressed this issue in its early stages, we would not have created a culture where employees took workplace equipment for granted.

Values Dialogues

Sanjay: In order to promote a culture of values in my own team, I was thinking of introducing some kind of reward system. But later, I found out that here in our organization, we do not reward values-oriented conduct and behaviour but only reward business outcomes. Would it not be a good idea to reward values-based conduct?

Sheela: Both reward and punishment in the context of values have always been subjects of debate. I don't believe any conclusion is really possible on this; that is to say that it is not possible to conclusively arrive at a verdict on whether we should or should not reward or punish conduct, behaviour or work based on values.

Sanjay: But almost all aspects of any business organization work on the basis of reward and punishment.

Sheela: Not really. Let us take the subject of quality. A couple of decades ago, I was part of a company where we had a very detailed study on whether or not we should reward an employee for the quality of the work performed. We even put some monetary rewards in place. But we soon had some situations where people began to question whether the task was performed to high quality or was it just the expected quality. We went through a period of uncertainty and debate.

Sanjay: And in the case of values, this confusion will be further amplified.

Sheela: Exactly. The following are some of the questions that will get asked: He was truthful in that scenario; why didn't you recognize that? She did not bend the rules for company profits; why wasn't she rewarded? It can get very messy.

Sanjay: But violations do get punished, don't they? For example, it was found that in my accounts of travel expenses there were some minor discrepancies. The organization did not take it kindly, even though it was a genuine mistake on my part and not a deliberate act to make some money.

Sheela: Yes, there are certain violations, which most organizations treat with utmost seriousness. Depending on the culture of the organization, the tolerance levels are very low towards many of the violations, in areas like accounts, finance, IP, respect for others, etc.

Sanjay: So organizations do punish employees for violations?

Sheela: Yes, but it is not black and white in all cases. It depends on the culture of the organization, and the organization's commitment to values. Punishment in the case of violations or transgressions sends a clear message regarding the organization's stance and commitment to values. And punishments need not always mean being asked to resign. It could range from a simple verbal warning to a strong legal action. Remember, episodes of punishments also become stories in the organization and serves to reinforce the culture of values in the organization. It sends a clear message across the organization, a message that is free from ambiguity.

Sanjay: But in the case of upholding values, it is what the policy of the organization is, and that is how we are expected to act. Hence, there is no reward. Is that the reasoning?

Sheela: You can say that. But this is also not a universal stance. There are organizations where values-based conduct is recognized but may not be rewarded. These instances find a mention in the organization's communications. In one of the organizations I had worked with, there was an instance when a customer asked the account manager who was handling the account to do some adjustments in the invoicing to save some taxes. This could have been easily done and would have gone well with the customer. But the account manager took a stance and said that it would be inappropriate. This episode was talked about a lot to reinforce the organization's values.

Sanjay: In summary, this is a very subjective point—reward, recognition or punishment. Though I don't have an absolute answer to my question, I understand the line of thinking and will take it up further with my boss.

Values Reflection

Introspect and deliberate upon these questions as you go forward in strengthening your organization's culture of values:

- What challenges have you faced, at your individual level, in the context of instilling values in your organization?
- What are the values (principles, Code of Conduct, etc.) that have been identified as the foundation to your organization's culture?
- How would you describe the success of instilling values in your organization?
- What measures have been taken at the senior management level in your organization to instil and cultivate values?
- What are the instances where you have seen violations of the identified values? Why do you think such violations occur?
- What are the subtle values violations that you have observed in your team and do you see this trend spreading beyond your immediate team?

* * *

उद्यमेन हि सिध्यन्ति कार्याणि न मनोरथैः ।
न हि सुप्तस्य सिंहस्य प्रविशन्ति मुखे मृगाः ॥

Any work is accomplished only by perseverance and continued effort, and not by mere wishes and desires. By themselves, deer certainly do not enter the mouth of a sleeping lion.

—Subhaashitam

10 Chapter

BUILDING THE CITADEL

> *Character is what you are when you are all alone,*
> *what you do when there is no one around to impress. It*
> *has been said that the measure of someone's character is*
> *what they would do if they never would be found out.*
>
> **—Greg Laurie**

Values Are the Foundation

When it comes to setting up a business, where do we begin? A typical response would be—business plan and vision. Think again.

Values are the most fundamental ingredient (Figure 10.1). When one or more individuals come together and wish to collaborate to create anything, it cannot be achieved without values. Most often, we do not state them explicitly, but they do exist. That is why the organization is born.

What we wish to reiterate is that the leaders of the organization need to consciously recognize that values are crucial and that they need to nurture these values across the organization, founding a culture that is based on a deep commitment to values.

Values are what comes even before the organization's vision, and the very first business plan.

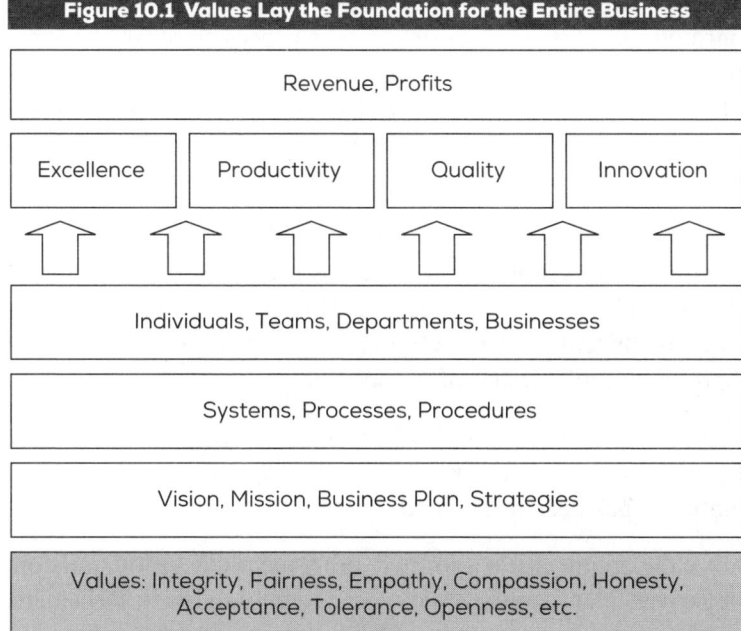

Figure 10.1 Values Lay the Foundation for the Entire Business

Revenue, Profits

| Excellence | Productivity | Quality | Innovation |

Individuals, Teams, Departments, Businesses

Systems, Processes, Procedures

Vision, Mission, Business Plan, Strategies

Values: Integrity, Fairness, Empathy, Compassion, Honesty, Acceptance, Tolerance, Openness, etc.

What if the organization already exists? Yes, it is never too late. The leaders and senior management need to come together and identify the values which are very crucial, not only for their survival but also to take the organization to higher levels of growth.

What Comes First—Ambition or Values?

Since we are discussing values in the context of an organization, the natural question one may ask is 'Does the organization's goals come first or do values come first?'

Any organization comes into existence because of an idea held by one or more individuals. Needless to say, the idea comes first coupled with a vision of an organization. However, the individuals come together because there is a basic match of frequency among them.

What is this frequency match? It can be seen as an alignment or harmony of certain ideas or thought processes regarding what the individuals wish to achieve. This includes an alignment of values. So it is fair to say that when the founders of the organization come together with business ideas, there is at some level (maybe unstated) an alignment of values.

But what is the basic driver for the organization? Clearly it is the organization's vision. Or at least it is the collective ambition of the individuals coming together. This is what the individuals state as objectives of the organization in the Memorandum of Agreement and Articles of Association.

So to put to rest that point, when two or more individuals come together with a collective dream, the organization's vision or ambition has been articulated.

Once the organization is formed, other ideas like vision, mission, objectives, plan, strategy, policy, etc., get established. Depending on the organization, some or all of these may be drafted.

What is important in this context is not what terms are used to define the 'organization's dream and ambition' but that it is shared by the various individuals in the organization. Instead of using all these or some of these words, let us use the term purpose to define the organization's vision, mission, etc.

Shared Purpose

Instead of just the founders carrying the purpose of the founders, it is now shared across the organization to make it a shared purpose of the organization.

The moment we have a shared purpose for the future, a new organization is born. So instead of each of the individuals having an ambition or a dream, all of them share a common purpose of taking the organization into the future.

If you examine the family as a microcosm of the organization scenario, here too, the way each of the parents think about each other's aspirations and ambitions is very different from what they want from the family as a unit. That shared purpose will also drive how the children are brought up.

In essence, for the organization to succeed (whatever the word success means—revenue, profits, market share, impact on society, etc.), the most fundamental things are for the employees of the organization to have a shared purpose. The organization moves forward successfully, if at least a reasonable number of the employees share that common purpose or vision. If everybody thinks differently, then there is a problem.

It doesn't mean that day to day, the organization will not achieve what it set out to achieve. That is because the organizational machinery is in place. So the manufacturing unit, for example, will still churn out 100 units a day.

But for the overall vision or purpose to be achieved consistently over a period of years and also for the organization to move ahead with changes in the industry, economy, etc., many in the organization must share that purpose.

Coming back to the case of the family, the children will grow up, get educated, find good jobs, get married, have children, etc., but it may not be necessarily the vision that you, as parents, had envisioned. These would have happened anyway in the natural course.

For the organization to be successful, that shared purpose is very crucial. With what sincerity the employees hold that shared purpose will matter in the long run. If Apple is generating the kind of innovation, products and quality decade after decade, it is not likely to happen unless a critical mass share that vision of design, quality and technical excellence.

The Stages of Instilling the Vision

Having said that a shared purpose is the starting point for the organization, how to make that happen? How do we realize that vision? Isn't that the next natural question?

Sharing the purpose with the employees of the organization is a part of the process of achieving that purpose or vision. More and more studies are revealing that this is in fact a very crucial factor in the success of any organization. As an organization grows in size, the number of people who share that vision keeps going down. It may not be so numerically, but the critical mass goes down unless some deliberate measures are taken to bring everyone to become part of that organizational purpose, including those who are joining the organization along the way.

Do people across all levels of the organization share that vision? During the organization's journey, many individuals join and also some leave from time to time. Given this constant churn, instilling the shared purpose in all employees remains a constant challenge and requires attention.

In the case of any organization, following are the stages of instilling the shared purpose:

Stage 1: Create a shared purpose statement; verbalize the same

Stage 2: Understand the shared purpose

Stage 3: Get inspired by the shared purpose (create a spark)

Stage 4: Instil the shared purpose into the DNA of the organization

Often people get inspired when they are introduced to the vision of the organization, particularly when it is presented well in person. So the spark of inspiration has happened, but the spark fails to stay. That's where most organizations fail. That spark has not been translated into the DNA of the organization. How the organization achieves this depends on the culture of the organization.

Essentially, the point here is 'Does the organization's purpose become every individual's purpose?' (Obviously in the context of the organization.) Or 'Does the vision stay with a handful of founders of the organization?'

Inspiration is very momentary. To retain the inspiration is the challenge. Do employees live that inspiration?

Consider a scenario: Elon Musk says, 'We will be the first to take people to Mars'. Everyone is instantly charged and feels the spark. But does it become a shared purpose for all employees in the organization. Leadership plays a critical role here.

In most cases, the organization is not doing enough to translate that inspiration into the organization's DNA.

At times, organizations such as NASA, Amazon, HP and IBM all have gone through this journey, when most employees in the organization, if not everybody, are at the same frequency. They seem to be resonating like a great soccer team at its peak performance.

The famous McKinsey 7S Framework—a management model developed by Robert H. Waterman, Jr. and Tom Peters—has shared values at its very core.

Instilling Values through Osmosis

In the initial years of a business, almost all organizations have no formal or written statements regarding values of the organizations.

To begin with, even the founders have not consciously thought of the idea of values that are essential for building the organization. When a group of founders come together and set up an organization, the values they embody collectively become the de facto values for the organization. These are the values that enabled them to come together, apart from, of course, the core idea behind the formation of the entity. The dominant values among them tend to become the dominant values of the team and the organization, at least in the initial stages.

At that stage of the business, as individuals come into the organization, they naturally adopt the prevailing values. Following are some very important points to note regarding the prevailing conditions:

- No one tells you what the values are.
- There are no written documents.
- There is no orientation programme.

- The entire focus of all is on getting the business on firm ground.
- In many cases, even the idea of values is not perceived as something critical at that juncture.

Then how do the new recruits receive the values? It is through the process of osmosis—gradual absorption through mingling with others in the organization. The more the founders interact and mingle with the new entrants, the more is the opportunity for the new joinees to absorb the values.

With time, many of the employees may embody a common set of values, which begin to define the character of the organization in terms of the following: transparency and speed in decision-making, integrity in dealing with vendors and customers, concern for employees, etc.

Because of the relatively small size of the organization, it is relatively easy for the values to permeate and pervade the entire team, without any need for having to declare and communicate them formally.

Possible Dilution of Values

At some later point in time, as the organization grows in size (in terms of people and business), it begins to sense some dilution in the value orientation.

The following is one possible explanation of what happens: the distance between the majority of employees and the founding team increases. Here, the distance can be interpreted in either of the following ways:

- There are too many levels (in the hierarchy) separating the majority and the founders.
- There are just too many employees, and there is not enough interaction of the majority with the founding team.

Essentially, the process of osmosis is hindered or interrupted. As the size of the organization grows (Figure 10.2), there is greater possibility of dilution in the culture of values.

Even in the initial stage of the organization, say when the organization grows in size, from 25 to 100 employees, care needs to be taken to immediately do the following:

- Continue the interactions between the employees and founders.
- Formalize the process of identifying and instilling the values that form the foundation of the organization.
- Create processes for constant interactions between the senior management and junior-level employees.

Figure 10.2 Growth of an Organization and Dilution

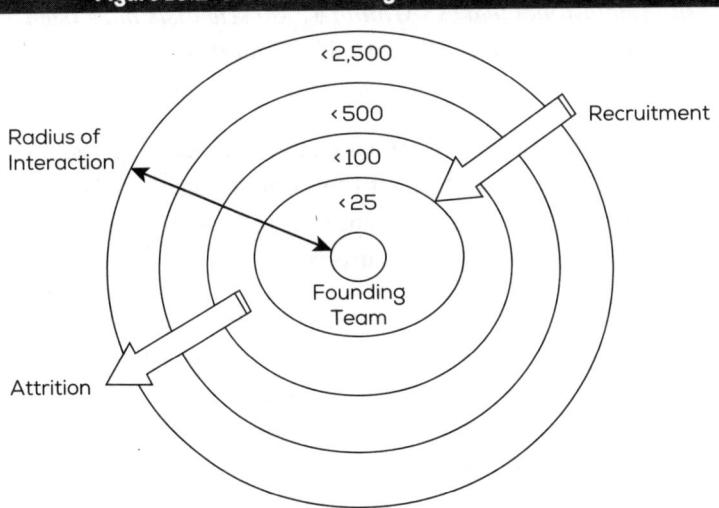

Note: The numbers used are just indicative to show different stages of growth.

Depending on the culture, nature of business and, above all, leadership, certain organizations are able to transition from one phase to another without dilution.

In many organizations, as the radius of interaction (distance between the founding team/senior leadership and front line of the organization) increases, there is a tendency for the values to be diluted.

Constant vigil regarding values is the key to sustaining the culture of values.

Everyone Shares a Purpose—What Next?

Let's take a scenario: A and B are space scientists. Both A and B individually share the vision of the organization. But for the rocket to go up, all the scientists have to pool their resources (expertise, experience, etc.) and come together to make it happen.

Think about this:

The 2017 Nobel Prize for Physics was awarded to Rainer Weiss, Barry C. Barish and Kip S. Thorne for contributions to the LIGO detector and the observation of gravitational waves. Around 1,000 scientists have been at it for the last 40 years. How did this happen? How did this coordination take place?

Next important question is: What enables this 'coming together'? What are the nuts and bolts of this coming together? When we say coming together, we are referring to coming together as a cohesive team for a common purpose.

This is what we are calling 'values', and this is the subject of this book. These nuts, bolts and oil of this coming together of individuals to achieve a common objective is what values are all about. It doesn't matter what you call these nuts and bolts—principles, Code of Conduct, values.

The phrase 'coming together' is not only used in the context of achieving a long-term vision of the organization but also applied to day-to-day business transactions and even meetings.

Take the example of Mumbai *dabbawalas* (those who deliver the lunch boxes), who have been delivering lunch boxes since 1890. If the dabbawalas have to be effective, there is a set of values that holds all these individuals together to make the system work like a well-oiled machine.

Similar is the case with the 5,000 dabbawalas, who deliver without fail, every day. This would not be possible unless the commitment was at the individual level.

What we are discussing is summarized by what Netflix claims about its culture:

> What is unique and special about Netflix is how much we:
> - encourage independent decision-making by employees
> - share information openly, broadly and deliberately
> - are extraordinarily candid with each other
> - keep only our highly effective people
> - avoid rules

Source: https://jobs.netflix.com/culture (accessed on 9 April 2019)

People, Not Process

The mistake we make often is to stop at the level of process or a system, saying that the process ensures excellence or performance. The real secret of teams lies with the individuals.

Process is a high-level definition of what is to happen. But for the process to be effective, the individuals' application, diligence and commitment, etc., all have to be in place. We can fulfil the process to the letter and still not achieve the objective.

The question to ask is 'Who makes the process happen?' If there are five individuals who are participants in a process, each one has to interpret the process properly and go beyond the written process guidelines for effectively meeting the end objective and going beyond.

That is where values come in. So it is not the processes that seal the whole deal. It is what values each of those participants bring to the table. In other words, the process depends on the attitude of each of the players involved in the process.

Perhaps that is the reason why Netflix says, 'Our core philosophy is people over process'.

Does It Take Many Years to Implement?

Values are thought of as something that will yield results, if at all, in the long run. So most managers feel that it doesn't make sense here and now in the business context.

You may recall, this was the attitude of the business organizations towards the idea of quality in the early years of adoption of quality as an important factor in business.

Let's look at Bridgewater Associates, the biggest hedge fund company in the world, founded by Ray Dalio. At some point, they decided that they will be guided by certain principles in their organization's journey. One of their core values is transparency, which they took to great heights. They didn't achieve that level of transparency, which some call 'radical', in one day. They started, however, with a small single step.

Even if it is induction of a new skill in the organization, it takes its own course. It begins with one step.

Where Do We Begin?

The first question the organization has to think about is 'Are you clear that the organization has to address the subject of values now, in order to build a suitable organizational culture, for meeting its business needs?'

If the answer to the question is 'yes', then what are you going to do about it?

The fact is that you have created an organization. The organization did not come up in a day. What you have built did not happen overnight. Organically, things happened and the organization has been moving forward.

Based on some observations or feedback, you—as management—realize that certain aspects of the organization need some fine-tuning. This suggests that the organization culture has imbibed the value of being open to feedback and correction.

What is important to note is that the organization examining the subject of values does not mean that the organization and its culture are devoid of values. It just means that going forward there are some other aspects of the organization's culture that will be addressed very consciously. So the journey is all about strengthening and/or fine-tuning the values.

If you have a vision of building an organization which hopes to sustain itself successfully in the long run, then there is no option but to create an organizational culture that is founded on values.

No one has refuted this point.

Why Should We Strive for Creating a Values-Based Environment?

It seems rather strange that we have to justify the need for being values based. In our discussions, this was an alarming point. This itself shows the condition of our society.

Based on the study, the following points clearly state why one should seriously consider the proposition of a values-based organization:

- As we have seen in an earlier section, the problem of fraud or values violation can hit every function/area/department of the organization.
- What starts as minor violations can slowly spiral into larger transgressions, which can lead to an irreparable crisis, which can permanently damage the reputation of the organization. This has been seen in the case of many organizations.
- Lack of values in the organizational context creates a very unhealthy work culture, which results in attrition. It is very difficult to retain good talent in such an environment.
- The very purpose with which the organization was set up is vitiated, if there is a violation of values.

Three fundamental points to contemplate upon are as follows:

- There is no choice in the matter.
- This is our true nature.
- It is our responsibility towards fellow citizens, family members, colleagues and friends.

A Framework for Building a Values-Based Organization

Some key points you have to remember:

- The subject of values is very closely tied to the culture of the organization.
- It is a very nebulous and subtle subject for implementation.
- Identify the values and plan implementation based on the culture of your organization.

Any attempt to suggest a framework would be a presumptuous one. However, based on our discussions with organizations, we examine here some generic aspects of the implementation.

- *Intent:* This is the birth of an idea of creating a values-based organization, and an expression of intent to take it forward. This recognition could be based on some study or analysis of the organizational culture while trying to address some problems in the area of productivity, quality, innovation, well-being, etc. It is important to clearly articulate why the organization would like to create an organizational culture based on values. This clarity of intent is most crucial to how you proceed in this journey. This could be done at the time of founding the organization or at some other point in time. This has to be aligned with the organization's vision, mission and objectives.

- *Resolve:* Acceptance of the intent by the entire senior management and a resolve to implement this across the organization is of paramount importance. This also ensures the buy-in from all members of the senior management. This is the time to bring everyone on the same page with regards to the journey of values. From time to time, new members would be inducted to the senior leadership team. It is very critical that at all times, all the members of the leadership team are unanimous with regard to the values and their role in building the organization.

- *Identification:* Identify the values that will form the backbone of the organization's culture and also clearly articulate the values to make them free from ambiguity. The contexts of each of the values, their definition, their role in organization building, etc., have to be clearly understood and articulated. There is a need to establish a common vocabulary. We will deal with the subject of identification of values in more detail later in this chapter.

- *Communication:* This is an ongoing activity to keep the entire organization clearly informed of the importance of values, the core values and their definition and manifestation. Since every organization constantly undergoes changes by way of attrition, recruitment, new businesses, new departments, etc., it is important that constant communication is carried out to keep the focus on values.

Real-life stories regarding organizational experiences have been found to be an excellent way to communicate the meaning and importance of values at the workplace. The stories that talk of how a certain individual or team acted in a manner upholding the organization's values are a very effective way to communicate, demonstrate and reinforce values. At the same time, stories of values violations and how these violations were dealt with serve to reiterate what values mean to the organization. Most of our respondents have stressed on the importance of stories on culture building in their organizations.

- *Instilling values:* Instilling values, living values, introspecting over the organizational culture periodically and of course taking remedial action are an ongoing cycle. The most crucial aspect of this journey of values is for everyone to 'live values'. There is no substitute to that.

- *Feel the pulse:* Individual values are often not perceptible in the day-to-day life of the organization. But if there is a violation, we immediately notice it. The culture and well-being of the organization give an indication of the extent to which values have been instilled in the organization. The quality of leadership at all levels can be assessed by the ability to feel the pulse of the organization and also being able to prevent values violations.

Following are some of the ways organizations have been getting a sense of the status of values in them:

- *Informal chats:* This is perhaps the easiest and the most common way of getting to understand the extent to which values have pervaded the organization. This involves senior management members informally talking to employees across different departments, levels and locations. These are not planned, and extremely casual, so that employees are in a free frame of mind and chat casually. These are not necessarily led by an agenda. In some organizations, senior management gives a lot of importance to these coffee-machine chats, as they bring out what people actually feel about the culture of the organization and also offer critical feedback about the way the organization is managed. If you feel that the employees are not talking freely during such sessions, that too is an important feedback to address. That too is an indicator of the culture of the organization.

- *Open houses:* Also referred to as town halls, this is a practice in some of the organizations. Many organizations begin this activity, but not every organization is able to sustain it effectively. This is a forum where employees are free to ask any questions, give feedback and raise grievances regarding the organization's functioning, business, their area of work, etc. A senior executive from an IT service organization said that although such sessions are extremely useful in creating an open culture, they are quite challenging. The crucial thing in these is to be able to follow up on the points raised and stand by your commitments to the employees in the earlier sessions.

- *Exit interviews:* When any employee resigns from the organization, the exit interviews with HR department or managers or senior management (depending on the processes in the organization) can be a very important source for gathering feedback about the culture of the organization. In such session, most of the time individuals are very open and free, as they are free from any threats of repercussion. Some individuals could also go to extremes in providing feedback, so these inputs have to be carefully examined.

- *Interactions with managers:* Some organizations have a very effective system whereby feedback from employees which go to their immediate managers go up the organization's hierarchy in a very effective and constructive manner. This is often part of the training provided to the managers where they are encouraged to keep the management posted about any feedback relating to the culture of the organization.

Identifying Values

Here, we present various perspectives to how we can go about identifying values. Examining these different perspectives might encourage you to create your own approach based on how your organization has been approaching any new initiative. Remember these are just suggestions, based on experiences elsewhere. You will have to figure out what works for you based on your own past experiences and prevailing culture.

Perspective 1

This is a simple approach which examines the different aspects of the organization's role to the business, employees, customers, society, etc. Addressing each of the following areas and performing a detailed 'what-enables-it' analysis will lead you to the values that the organization needs to adopt.

- Core values: We have already discussed this earlier in the book, for example, integrity, empathy, compassion, etc.
- Qualifications of products or services: These are attributes that further qualify your product or service, and these

are aimed at providing you an edge over competition, for example, deliver 'wow' through service.

- Qualities that define how you approach work: These qualities define how all the employees approach work and performance. These go a long way in creating a culture where there is a constant endeavour to improve productivity, creativity and quality, for example, do more with less.

- Responsibility towards each other: These values reflect the commitment and responsibility towards each other in the organization and contribute to the well-being of the employees at the workplace, for example, we respect each other's point of view.

- Commitment to adhere to the law of the land: This component defines the policies, systems and procedures that define the organization's commitment to conform to the law of the land in all aspects of the organization's function.

- Responsibility towards environment: Some organizations also state their commitment and responsibility to the environment as part of their principles, for example, protect trees.

- Responsibility towards the society and the nation: This provides the guiding light to the organization regarding each employee's commitment to the society and the nation. This also includes the commitment of the employees and the organization towards their customers, vendors and other external agencies, for example, no forced labour or child labour.

Perspective 2

Any organization which decides to adopt ethics and values in its culture needs to examine the implementation at different levels.

Figure 10.3 gives an overview.

	Figure 10.3 Values Hierarchy	
5	Values that enhance the effectiveness of the individual in the organization	Individual
4	Values that enhance the effectiveness of different functions	Function/Team
3	Core values that uniquely identify the character of the organization	Organization
2	Adherence to industry/sector-specific values/ethics/norms	Industry
1	Values that ensure adherence to the Law of the Land (by the organization)	Nation

1. Law of the land: The most fundamental and mandatory aspect of ethics and values for any organization is to ensure that the organization does not violate the laws of the land. No organization has a choice in this regard. Towards this end, it has to have the necessary policies, systems and processes.

2. Industry norms: Any industry will have norms typically laid down by regulatory agencies which establish norms and standards for a particular industry or sector.

3. Organization's values: Any organization has its own culture which defines the principles and values that govern its business, operations and interactions within the organization and outside, in relation to customers, vendors and other external agencies. This, in other words, defines the character of the organization. In general, these are identified when the organization is founded; however, it may formally come into existence, at a later point in time, in some cases.

These values also establish the position and status of the organization in the eyes of the employees, customer, vendors and competitors. In most organizations, these are formally documented and made available to all the stakeholders and form a part of different communications within and outside the organization.[1]

4. Function level values: Different functions across any organization require different skills and attitudes in the employees. The R&D function requires different attitudes, while the accounts function requires a different orientation. It is for the organization to recognize and nurture function-specific values for the different functions and teams.

   Values such as integrity, acceptance, trust, empathy and flexibility may require greater emphasis in a team involved in designing products and services. Whereas a team involved in administration and logistics may need greater emphasis on a different set of values.

   Also, here the focus of values is not so much to adhere to some norms, or laws or regulations but to enhance the effectiveness of the individuals and teams to achieve their milestones and targets and improve upon them.

5. Individual: All values—organizational or departmental—need to be translated to the individual level values. Finally, any value is instilled and upheld only at the level of the individual.

   We can divide values into two broad categories: (a) those that enable the organization and its functions to adhere to the law and such other norms; (b) those that enhance the effectiveness of individuals to perform better.[2]

---

[1]For the first three levels, the codes that define these values/ethics are well-defined and documented.

[2]Only when all these different levels are synchronized, the implementation of ethics and values will be complete and comprehensive.

Perspective 3

The organization need not start with all the values. To begin with, the focus may be restricted to a few. The experience with them will prepare the organization to take on more, which can be gradually included.

Figure 10.4 gives some hints regarding where to begin. Values like cleanliness, order, non-wasting, etc., relate to the physical space around us. These are relatively easy to follow and demonstrate. They are also tangible and visible. In all, it gives a good place to make a beginning (Japanese 5S philosophy also reflects this view).

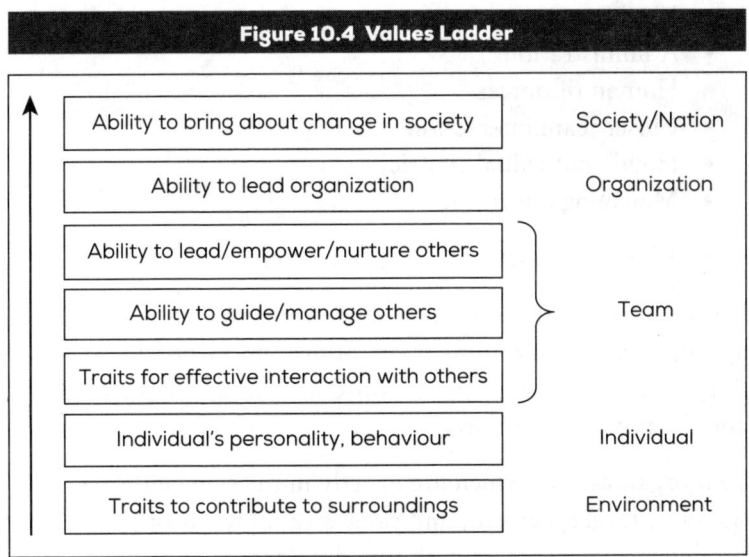

Figure 10.4 Values Ladder

These are mere guidelines. There are no clear boundaries among these. The idea of gradually enhancing the focus and circle of influence is for the organization to grow in its ability to instil and live these values and internalize them sufficiently before taking on more.

Perspective 4

Different types of jobs may involve different values to make us more effective at what we do. Suppose a job involves managing a number of machines and ensuring maximum throughput, then many of the values which relate to interpersonal interaction may not be relevant. There will be other values—which enhance one's own commitment and productivity at work—that need to be focused upon. Depending on the role or function, different values may play a crucial role.

Here is one other viewpoint where the choice of values depends on the nature of the individual's role and responsibilities:

- Customer-centric
- Vendor-centric, centred around government and other agencies
- Machine operations, factory operations
- Administration
- Human resources
- Closer team interaction
- Highly individual-centric
- Managing a team

To conclude this discussion on perspectives:

Needless to say, these are just suggestions that hint at possible approaches organizations may adopt in identifying values. But the approach will depend on the organization's leadership and the prevailing culture.

Two organizations which are exactly in the same industry, with the same target segment, and same size (in terms of people and revenues), may come up with two different set of values as their foundation for building their culture of values.

From the outside, it may be difficult to say, this is a good set of values or the right set of values or this is not a suitable set of values.

What is important is that the collective leadership, taking into account the prevailing culture, sets out to identify the core values. Since this is a journey forever, this would be an iterative one and you may not necessarily get it right the first time.

Identifying Values Based on Functions—A Simple Example

Let us examine the role of a manager and see which values play a key role. Doing a what-enables-it analysis, we find that any manager, in order to be able to carry out the responsibilities effectively, must be able to:

- Understand what motivates the different members of the team.
- Sense the problems faced by the individual team members.
- Understand the obstacles team members are facing in fulfilling their responsibilities.
- Anticipate and avoid interpersonal issues among team members.
- Understand why certain team members are conducting themselves in a certain way, which is resulting in a dip in the productivity of the entire team.
- Understand which aspects of work give them joy and which demotivate them.
- Sense why the productivity of a certain team member has fallen.

Again, let us ask the question, 'What enables it?'

The one value that is of paramount importance for the manager is empathy.

Here is what a project manager with an IT services company in India had to say, citing a situation where the values of empathy, camaraderie and trust (among his teammates) generated a deep sense of gratitude towards his boss, his team and the entire organization:

My mother had to undergo surgery, and this came about all of a sudden. I had no time to apply for leave or hand over my work to someone else. I barely managed to inform my boss too. It was almost a two-week absence from workplace, and there was no concept of working from home then. I couldn't devote time to figure out what was going on at work, and how they were managing with what I was supposed to do. I had the complete support of my boss and the entire team, and I could devote all my energy and attention to the family. And when I came back, I was all inspired and charged, and sprung back into action with a lot of energy and commitment. I could even notice a substantial enhancement in my productivity at work.

How Do Employees Perceive the Culture of Values?

For the purpose of implementation of a culture of values, it is important to understand how employees respond to different aspects of what the organization attempts to do. In fact, nothing can be achieved if you do not understand the employee perspective and take that into account, particularly in the context of culture building.

Needless to say, not all employees will see things in the same way. In reality, each employee has his/her own view on matters. But that would be an impractical approach when the organization's size is large.

For the purpose of the discussion, let us categorize the employees depending on their experience and seniority (Table 10.1). Note that the categorization here has been done only from the point of view of implementation of a culture of values. Also, depending on the prevailing culture in your organization and the demographics, you may consider a categorization that is appropriate to your context.

Only point to be kept in mind is that if the categorization is too fine (i.e., creating many categories), then the study can become very complicated and the subsequent implementation very impractical.

Table 10.1 Understanding People in the Organization					
	Perception of Episodes	**Perception of Decision-Making**	**Reaction to Values Violations**	**Face Values Conflicts or Dilemmas**	**Give Feedback**
Work Experience 0–5 Years					
5–10 Years					
Greater than 10 Years					
Managers					
New Recruits (With Experience)					
Temporary Staff					

Why do we need this kind of a matrix?

Organization, when working on various initiatives, sees employees en masse and refer to them as people. But we have to realize that each individual is different in terms of skills, capabilities, character, personality, etc. So in the context of initiatives— particularly those relating to the culture of the organization—it is important to understand the employees as individuals (with a personality), rather than seeing them as one homogeneous whole and addressing them as people.

However, from the point of view of planning, and figuring our systems and processes relating to values, it may not be pragmatic to take each individual into account. However, as a manager, he/ she will have to take each individual team member into account. Hence, we categorize the employees into some categories, so that we explore how different approaches are required for each of those categories of individuals. This primarily stems from the fact that our worldview is different at different points in our lives.

The point to remember is that this is not a worksheet to be filled in as a one-time exercise. This is primarily a means to understand that different approaches are required to address different individuals. This will change for each organization.

The analysis arising through the aforementioned categorization will help the organization address the following:

- How to articulate the values?
- What strategy to adopt for communication of values?
- How to strengthen the culture of values?
- What fine-tuning is required in the case of certain values?
- How to respond to values violations?
- How to gather feedback regarding the culture?
- What is a more appropriate decision-making process for this culture?

The following are another set of attributes that might help in the categorization of employees:

- Nature of work (accounts, design, manufacturing, etc.)
- Regional culture and customs in the country where the group is present

Temporary staff: Many organizations across industries engage temporary staff for different functions. Some of them even have a large percentage of temporary staff. In such cases, how does the organization sustain the culture of values or sustain any culture for that matter. In such cases, the only way to sustain a culture is to introduce the cultural elements (including those relating to values) into their systems and processes. For example, take the case of a fast-food chain, where empathizing with the customer would be a core value. Here this value (of empathy) has to be incorporated into the standard operating procedures (may be even using technology) so that even if there are frequent changes to the staff at the counter, the system ensures customer care.

Junior-Level Employees

The youngsters in every organization form the future of the organization. In every generation of the organization, they are the ones that carry the business into the future.

Here we are using the phrase 'junior-level employee' to mean one who has recently made a beginning to his/her work life with an experience of less than five years. This segment of the organization becomes even more important in cases where the organization has a significant percentage of employee strength in this experience category.

This is an experience narrated to us by a young executive in a data analytics company in India.

I was just about six months into the organization and was part of an important project. We had another couple of months before the final date of completion of this project. But the programme manager suddenly announced that the customer wants it to be completed two weeks before the scheduled date. Some of us put in very long hours, and some did it in spite of family commitments. We still managed to complete the project as per the revised date. However, we got to know later from the programme manager that he had changed the date without any prompting from the customer, mainly to create a buffer. He said he was a little apprehensive whether we would meet the deadline, hence wanted to introduce some urgency. Many of us were shocked by this. Some of the team members had to undergo a lot of difficulties on the family front to fulfil their commitment to complete this task on time. I too was shaken by this.

Why is it important to understand and address employees with sensitivity and care?

- The experiences that take place in their work life now have a strong impact on their perception and influence their worldview, sometimes for life.
- The early experiences also have a deep influence in shaping their personality.
- If there are persistent experiences that have a negative impact, these impressions become very difficult to change.
- At the same time, positive influence can be a great contribution for their entire career.

How to Build Values-Based Organizations?

It might appear to be a very challenging endeavour for any organization to embark on this journey of creating a values-based environment. However, it is a very natural process and also an imperative.

Having resolved and committed to build a values-based organization, it is the ongoing harmonious interaction between management and employees that helps build and sustain an environment of values orientation in the organization.

As depicted in Figure 10.5, while the organization nurtures, facilitates and supports employees in their pursuit of fulfilling their responsibilities in a values-based manner, it is employees that form the building blocks of the values-based set-up.[3]

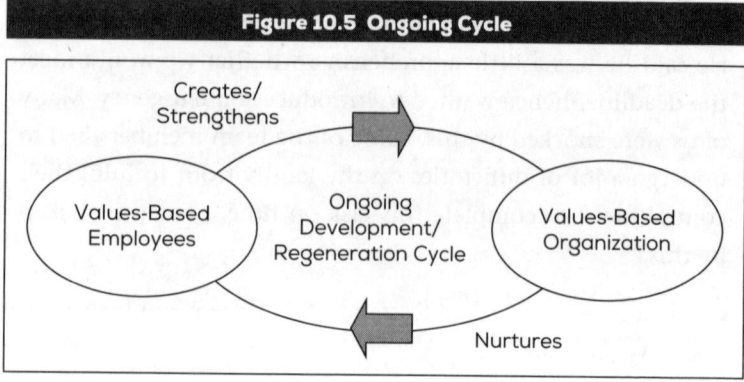

Figure 10.5 Ongoing Cycle

Needless to say, building a values-based culture begins with a sincere resolve by the founders and management of the organization to commit themselves to create a culture of values and also live those values. Figure 10.6 gives an overview.

---

[3]When we refer to employees or individuals in the context of the organization, it includes all individuals associated—members of the board, management team and other employees.

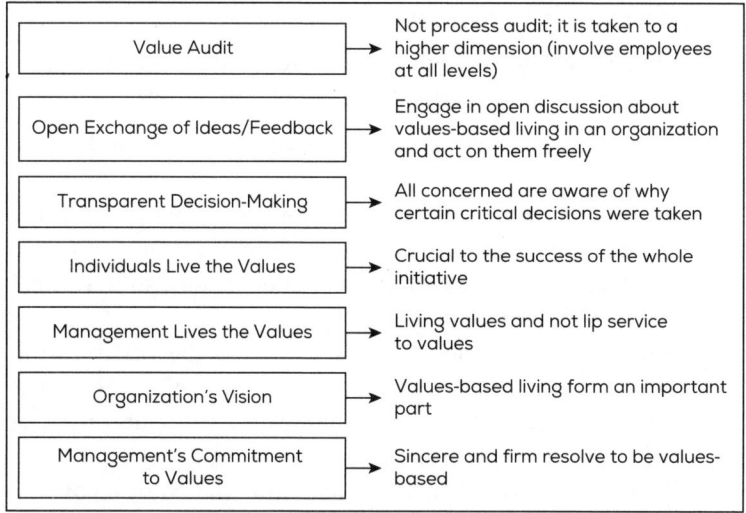

Figure 10.6 Creating a Culture of Values

Value Audit	Not process audit; it is taken to a higher dimension (involve employees at all levels)
Open Exchange of Ideas/Feedback	Engage in open discussion about values-based living in an organization and act on them freely
Transparent Decision-Making	All concerned are aware of why certain critical decisions were taken
Individuals Live the Values	Crucial to the success of the whole initiative
Management Lives the Values	Living values and not lip service to values
Organization's Vision	Values-based living form an important part
Management's Commitment to Values	Sincere and firm resolve to be values-based

It is very important for everyone to understand and keep in mind why we have adopted a culture of values orientation to govern every aspect of organizational functioning, that is, what is the purpose behind being values based.

Do Not Announce Your Values to the Customer

This is the policy that has been adopted by a medium-sized IT services organization for furthering the culture of values in the organization. This is based on the philosophy that 'actions speak more than words'. As a policy, they have not shared their values with anyone outside the organization, including customers and vendors. Most organizations take great pride in sharing their values in their communications brochure and website. But this organization has consciously decided not to do so, but all allow its actions to speak for themselves.

The idea of not sharing the list of values of the organization with customers also comes from its experience where people tend to offer more lip service and at times overstate these, while in their actions, they do not uphold them. This conflict and contradiction between speech and action leaves the customer (or any other external agency) in a state of extreme disappointment, a situation very hard to recover from.

In general, values-based organizations adopt the following practices regarding communication of values within the organization:

- Values of the organization are shared with the individual upon joining.
- Training programmes help in constantly reinforcing the values and their impact on the organization, and also emphasis is given to what each value means, so that there is a common understanding.
- Stories and episodes are shared across the organization which reinforces the importance of the values and their application, as also to communicate the commitment of the leadership towards these values.
- There are stories which highlight the stance of the management in dealing with violations of values.
- Recognition of instances where values were upheld under trying circumstances.

Key Points to Remember and Communicate

Based on our studies of values-based organizations, the following are some key messages to reinforce among employees in order to strengthen the culture of values:

We are not devoid of values; we need to strengthen them.

When we take up the issue of values in the organization, sometimes an incorrect signal that goes across is we are not values based today. That is a dangerous misconception. Because the moment we think like that, we are going to resist the idea of values. We are what we are because of values alone.

All that is required to be done is to go to the next level, that is, we need to improve, we need to grow and we need to strengthen the demonstration or living of values.

We are not denying the fact that values exist today. Everything in the organization is happening because of values.

We need to live values; not just talk about them.

Values are to be lived. Merely possessing the values does not benefit others, the organization or the society. We need to demonstrate it and need to apply it to every situation.

Merely offering lip service to the idea of values is detrimental to the organization. If there is a mismatch between talk and the walk, people lose faith in the idea of values. Any effort to repair the situation will be counterproductive.

Living values is the best way to instil values in others and to communicate the idea of values.

Values orientation is an internal benchmark and goal.

We may avoid making it part of the marketing communication. Because the moment we wish to share this information with customers, shareholders, etc., there comes the point of wanting to appear to be good, and this usually takes predominance over wanting to be values based for its own sake.

Most organizations do share their values in public domain. However, there are organizations that have consciously decided to keep this an internal goal for them to live by.

While this is for each organization to decide based on the prevailing culture, it is definitely something the organization must introspect over before taking a decision.

Mere vision statements do not create a culture of values-based living.

Processes, policies, audits, etc., do not ensure values-based conduct, interactions and a values-based culture.

Recall the late 1980s and early 1990s when 'quality' was the watchword. 'Standards and certifications' entered the scene. Everyone aspired for certifications relating to various standards and frameworks. Everything was governed by audits and assessments. ISO, SEI CMM, etc., became the sought-after ways of demonstrating quality. Corporate communication brochures highlighted their commitment to quality by listing all the standards they conformed to. What was the result?

Soon, in some cases, it was all about being 'certified', and not about 'quality'. The entire process of audit and assessments began to be questioned. This is because the goal became 'certification' and not 'quality'.

Merely having a well-stated vision statement does not guarantee values.

The purpose for the existence of the organization has to be given a lot of thought. That is what governs our actions at every level in the organization. This is what provides incentives to be values oriented.

Ensure the following:

- Clarity/openness in communication
- Transparency in decision-making
- Commitment to values-based culture at senior management levels
- Genuineness/sincerity of intent

Articulation of Organization's Values

While intent and identification of values is the first step in building a values-based organization, the articulation of the same is of paramount importance. The crispness and clarity with which the values are enunciated will go a long way in instilling and living of values.

Why is articulation of values important in the journey of values?

- It presents the shared values chosen by the organization with a clear description of what these values mean.
- It communicates the values to all concerned in various languages, if necessary. For example, PepsiCo's Global Code of Conduct is made available on the company website in more than 20 languages.
- Clear articulation ensures that there is no ambiguity in what a certain value means. All concerned should be able to interpret every value to mean the same thing.

Let us briefly examine the different aspects of the 'Core Values and Code of Ethics' document from Cognizant. These are

Good Values, Great Business

the different sections (the italicized phrases are as used by Cognizant):

Letter from the CEO: This expresses the commitment of the organization to all its employees, saying: 'This document summarizes our comprehensive ethics program and underscores our commitment to integrity and moral responsibility'. This also acts as an inspiration for the rest of the organization: an unwavering belief in doing the right thing and a commitment to doing the best work for our clients no matter where we are in the world.

Core values: This section captures the six core values of the corporation: transparency, passion, empowerment, collaboration, customer focus and integrity. This is preceded by this statement: 'Whether we're working in a development centre, on-site with our customers, in our corporate office, or in our everyday lives, we must be role models of integrity'.

Who must follow the code: This list begins with the directors, officers and employees, and includes even business partners and third-party representatives (collectively referred to as associates).

What do I need to do: This articulates the responsibility of all associates in general and the manager in particular. Through this, the organization tells the employees what is expected of them especially in the context of upholding the core values.

Getting help or reporting a possible violation: This gives employees information about what steps to be taken when encountering a violation with regard to the values. However, there are subtler violations (discussed in Chapter 9), which are at times difficult to express. Managers need to be sensitized and coached in sensing and dealing with these subtle violations.

Our ethics earn trust: In this section, the following four points are discussed in some detail: preventing corrupt activities, avoiding conflict of interest, never engaging in insider dealing, and creating and maintaining accurate and complete records.

We do business the right way: This section presents the codes of conduct regarding the customers in the context of business dealings.

Our responsibilities are clear: Here, the responsibilities regarding being a good corporate citizen, adherence to safety standards and the guidelines for political and lobbying activities are highlighted.

We take principled actions: The idea of ethical business practices are elaborated here, particularly regarding privacy, security of data, use of technology, safe keeping of company assets, communicating about Cognizant, and discrimination and harassment.

Waivers of this code: Importantly, there may arise special circumstances where some exceptions may be necessary to the stated codes of conduct. These are discussed here.

The idea of presenting the case was to highlight the importance of the need for a comprehensive approach in examining all aspects of articulation of a values document.

However, we would have liked to see a detailed discussion of how the core values, namely transparency, passion, empowerment, collaboration, customer focus and integrity, need to be understood in the context of the organization.

Living Values

Even though values have been identified and clearly documented, unless they are practised, the entire initiative has no meaning or purpose. Normally phrases like demonstrate values, practise values, adhere to values, etc., are used. But we find that the one phrase which best captures the intent is live values.

Living values includes instilling the intent of the values in oneself, and then practising it in letter and spirit. The idea of living values also conveys a naturalness in the process. The way living for us is a natural and subconscious process, living values has to be natural and subconscious.

All other phrases such as demonstration, practice and adherence indicate a certain effortfulness in this whole process. When values become part of the DNA of the organization and that of the employees of the organization, it becomes a very easy, effortless and natural way of life in the organization. Thus, truly evolves a culture of values.

A few important points that are associated with living values are as follows:

- There cannot be an external motivation to being values based; it is an inner conviction.
- Living values is not just about a checklist of do's and don'ts or rules of conduct.
- What values we value, and adopt and live by will depend on what we choose as our shared purpose in the organization.

There are many instances at work that test our commitment to living values. Following are a few indicative ones:

- When you do a rushed job on the deliverable you were working on
- What you tell the participants when you arrive late for a meeting
- What is the response to the supervisor when the job assigned was not completed on time
- Why you are not speaking up during meetings

In other words, there are numerous opportunities for introspecting over our actions, which will tell us how well we are doing in the area of living values.

The most crucial thing to remember is that when it comes to living values, it is not about proving it to another person. It is about what we tell ourselves that will provide us with the real answer.

Challenges

There are a number of potential challenges in the journey of creating a values-based organization. Each organization will have to discover, improvise and experiment in its own way along the journey. This will depend on the following:

- The industry
- Size of the organization
- Profile of the employees
- Age of the organization
- Prevailing organizational culture

Based on the points shared by individuals during our study, we have compiled the following for organizations to think about and discover their own answers:

- There has always been a debate on whether to reward values-based conduct. It is a very subjective issue. We need to examine the following points and decide based on the prevailing culture in the organization:

  o By rewarding values-based conduct, what is the message we will send across the organization?
  o By rewarding values-based conduct, what is the conduct we are eliciting from individuals across the organization?
  o How do we decide which behaviour/conduct to reward?
  o Are we in a position to unambiguously judge whether a particular behaviour/conduct/interaction/act is values-based or not?

- When there is a conflict between adherence to values and its impact on work (in the short term), how managers and management respond will play an important role defining how individuals take to values. There are various subtler aspects to values which require a lot of maturity on the part of managers and management to be able to address and resolve conflicts.
- To be able to assess a situation or action and impartially come to a conclusion may not be always possible. This again depends on profile of managers.
- How do we respond to values violations?

  o What will be our response at the individual level?
  o What will be our response at a team level?
  o What will be our response at the organizational level?

- How are we going to deal with this challenge from employees saying 'who are you to judge me'?
- How are we going to ensure that we live up to the vision?
- Should a person be evaluated on values, particularly in a manner where it affects his/her performance?
- What is the process of giving feedback when it comes to values?
- Zero tolerance may not always be the best solution to create a culture of values. Different organizations take different positions in this regard.
- How to deal with cynicism? We often hear the following whenever you talk of values:

  o Honesty does not pay
  o You cannot run a business being values based
  o Values are not practical
  o No one who has always been values based has been successful
  o Why should an organization get into my personal space?
  o It is not relevant to what I do at work. What matters is—'I deliver what I promise'.
  o I feel uncomfortable when I am being monitored on various other personal attributes.
  o People always ask: 'If I do this, what does it get me?'

Sustaining a Culture of Values in a Large Organization

What should the organization do to continue to remain values based, even as the size of the organization continues to rise? Let us examine the different areas an organization has to look into to sustain a culture of values. It is easy to begin something. Sustaining it is a challenge. Figure 10.7 highlights the areas an organization has to focus upon in order to sustain this ongoing journey of values.

We have discussed some of these aspects earlier in this chapter. Here we bring it all together. These different areas continue throughout the life of the organization.

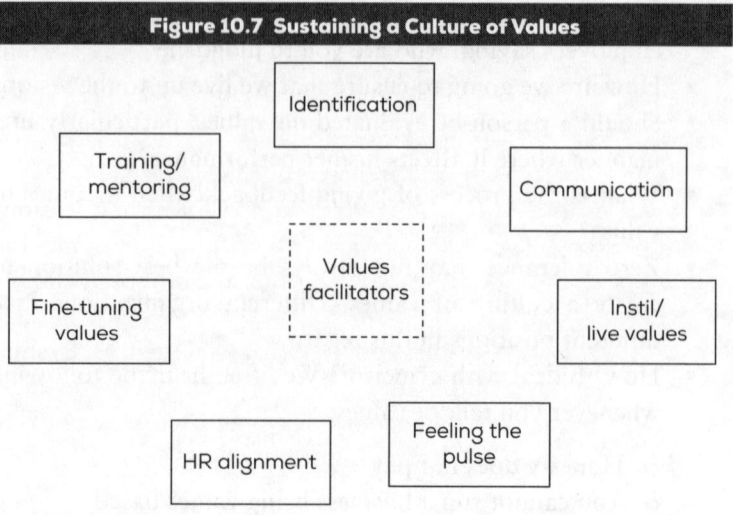

Figure 10.7 Sustaining a Culture of Values

Identification

Training/mentoring

Communication

Values facilitators

Fine-tuning values

Instil/live values

HR alignment

Feeling the pulse

Facilitators

Like all other endeavours, it is important that there is a team involved in carrying on this activity of managing the values movement in the organization. While the organization is small, this responsibility could be shared by individuals who are in other roles, but as the size of the organization grows, a team is necessary to sustain the values culture in the organization. In this context of having a team, you may draw parallels with the quality programme in the organization; and depending on that experience, create a similar facilitation team for driving and sustaining the values movement in the organization.

Feeling the Pulse

While the values get identified, articulated and communicated by the leadership of the organization, the adherence or deviations are felt first by front lines of the organization. All the senior leaders from different organizations we have spoken to felt that, attempted sincerely, it is easy to find out the extent to which values have pervaded the organization.

Here are some of the different approaches we came across adopted by organizations:

- Agenda-less meetings or informal chats of senior leadership with front lines are the easiest way to know to what extent values have pervaded the organization. This depends on the following:
  - Sincerity of intent on the part of the leadership
  - Casual nature of the interaction. Very formal sessions result in formal answers, which may not serve the purpose. Chatting freely results in the most valuable feedback
  - Extent of trust the employees have on their leadership
  - Outcomes and follow-ups from such past meetings. If there were no follow-ups in the past, it is unlikely anyone will give serious feedback
- Paying attention to the details of exit interviews (held when an employee quits the organization).
- Town hall meetings: Organizations which have such open meetings call them by different names. Such sessions are used as forums for communicating important organization developments and also for gathering feedback.
- Periodic meetings held at team and department levels also provide feedback, which are passed on by line managers to the senior management. This requires that there is a culture in the organization of front-line managers being receptive to feedback regarding organization culture and there is a process by which the feedback reaches the right teams/people for action. This input will have to be made part of what the orientation managers receive before they take over the role of a manager.
- Organizations sometimes initiate a mechanism of seeking feedback using questionnaire, which is an opportunity to gather feedback in a very comprehensive way. However, whenever feedback is gathered, the employees always expect some follow-up and action regarding the feedback given. The absence of follow-up action results in loss of faith in any such process of gathering feedback.

What is important to note is that if and when you find that people are not opening up and talking freely about the status of values in the organization, that itself is the first feedback which needs serious attention.

HR Alignment

HR has one of the most well-established processes in any organization. Following are some of the HR processes that can be aligned with the system of creating and sustaining the values culture in the organization.

- Recruitment: Recruitment of candidates who are aligned with the values of the organization is something most organizations do, even if they do not have a formal system of values. This becomes more crucial in senior roles.

  A senior management of a major transportation company in India said, 'We recruit a person not only for his/her experience, skill and attractive resume. We recruit a person for his/her value system. We may compromise on the skill or capability but not on the alignment of values'.

  Organizations find that it is easier to groom youngsters into their own values culture than seniors, as their years of experience have already reinforced their belief and value systems very strongly. In some organizations, at the time of joining, the new recruits are also made to sign certain documents relating to values and codes of conduct of the organizations.

- Orientation programme: The orientation programme is often the first opportunity where the new recruits get a detailed exposure regarding the values of the organization. This is best presented by one of the founders or by someone in the senior management team. This is also a great opportunity for clarifying any doubts and apprehensions the new recruits may have regarding the organization culture.

- Resignation: Typically, the HR department coordinates an exit interview upon resignation of an employee. This is seen as an opportunity to explore in detail the cause for the resignation. This is often the occasion when the employee opens up with feedback regarding various issues he/she may have had during one's tenure. This will include grievances or other feedback relating to the values of the organization. Often, individuals feel more comfortable bringing up their concerns regarding values violations during the exit interview than when they were still on the rolls of the organization for fear of any adverse reaction. This will also depend upon the culture of the organization. It is particularly important to deal with resignations of tenured staff who were well liked and known for being values oriented and their exit in some cases might be misinterpreted. Some organizations we know make it a point to send a very nice send-off e-mail to the entire staff wishing the person the best for their future.

Training and Mentoring

Ongoing training is an important means to create and sustain awareness about values in the organization. Most organizations have an established system of training across the year covering a wide range of subjects. Mentoring, which is also quite widely used to train and coach individuals, can also be used as a means to deal with subtler elements relating to upholding of values and how employees can deal with the conflicts and dilemmas relating to values. A well-known consulting firm we know has at least two internal programmes on ethics and values every year which each person is supposed to attend.

Conclusion

For an organization to come together, we need an inspiring vision, strong purpose and clear objectives. This cannot be the dream of just the founders or the senior management, it has to become a shared purpose or shared vision of all. For a shared purpose to get realized, all the individuals involved have to come together cohesively. And that coming together is enabled by what we call values. It is not the process definition and guidelines that make anything happen; it is the values all the individuals involved embody.

What applies to one organization may not apply to another in the same form. Based on the study, following are some pointers that can help:

- Lead by example. This is not just the responsibility of the management. It is each employee's responsibility. Each conduct and interaction of an individual can positively or adversely impact others around. Values adherence at the individual level is the bedrock of values-based organizations.
- Have regular communications regarding values—what they mean, how to seek help, inspiring messages, etc. These should not be impersonal communications.
- Bring in the right people who align with the culture of values.
- Demonstrate values adherence and more importantly live the values. Celebrate stories of adherence in tough circumstances.
- Facilitate values-based actions and decisions by providing the right environment.
- Do not use values orientation as a marketing 'tool', especially when internal reality is different.
- Invest more time in values orientation training and awareness. Any amount of time that is spent on this is a great service to society and also is a great contribution to the life of each individual and also goes beyond the confines of the organizational context.
- Continuously refresh and improve. It is a journey. Celebrate the past but be willing to change what is needed to. The recent example of Google rewriting its policies on sexual harassment (albeit under pressure from staff) is a powerful one. There may be a lot of unlearning involved; so be sensitive to it.

Values Dialogues

Sanjay: I have heard of instances from the past where we have taken punitive action against individuals who have violated certain core values and principles of the organization. Will fear not create an unhealthy atmosphere and hinder promotion of a values-based culture?

Sheela: It is not possible to give a yes or no answer to this question. Let us discuss the different aspects of implementation of values in an organization. The implementation consists of the following:

- Identification and unambiguous articulation of values and code
- Communication of these values to all concerned
- Policies regarding adherence and scope
- Policies regarding violations and resulting consequences
- System for looking into any violations and arriving at action

It is essential that the organization clearly articulates these points in the context of the organization and communicates them clearly. Many organizations ensure that the employee gets to know these points as part of the joining process, including signing appropriate documents in agreement of the same. In some others, these are let known to the employees as part of the orientation programme.

Sanjay: But, I don't think employees understand the gravity of these at the time of joining.

Sheela: It all depends on how these are communicated. Depending on how these are expressed and communicated, the organization may come across either as one which is waiting to punish each and every violation, or as a just and fair one.

Sanjay: When you see certain instances of punishment, particularly those that happen around you, then one becomes very apprehensive. Then there are all kinds of stories that start doing rounds. Then you become confused too.

Sheela: That depends on how transparently the issue is dealt with. I have heard of instances in an earlier organization, where very little was communicated to the employees about the whole episode. The only thing that everyone got to know was that so-and-so did something wrong, and hence this action. And the whole thing was executed in the course of just a couple of hours. Such haste leaves a lot of unanswered questions in the minds of employees, and that is very difficult to address later on.

Sanjay: I think people understand that there will be actions which will get punished harshly. For example, employees know the consequence of flouting secrecy laws with customers. So it is not that people do not understand.

Sheela: Absolutely. So it boils down to those five points we discussed earlier, and the transparency and grace with which these instances of violations are dealt with. Once people know these things, there is no question of living under fear. Let us consider the following scenario: you vanished for three days from work without informing anyone. You get back on the fourth day. You know you have done something which is unacceptable, particularly because you were supposed to complete and submit a report during that time. Of course, you may not get fired for this, but there will be some consequences, depending on the criticality of the report you were to submit. You would expect the management to take all things into account before judging you and taking action. You also expect that the management will hear your side of what happened. So even if you take this simple situation, there are ways of handling it elegantly and explaining your course of action to the employee without any ill feeling on anyone's part. At the same time, you could have someone just take off and say you need to be fired without even discussing the matter. Of course, I am giving this as an extreme response, but it is not unimaginable.

Sanjay: I feel the way the organization deals with such seemingly simple situations establishes how the employees see the management.

Sheela: Such instances, which we come across often, are what give the impression about the management. The organization being fair, transparent, empathetic, sincere, etc., is established by such instances. This quote by Greg Laurie comes to mind, 'Fear is a fine deterrent, and it has its place. But a better motive is wanting to do what is right'.

Values Reflection

Introspect and deliberate upon these questions, in the context of your organization, as you go forward in strengthening your organization's culture of values:

- List the top three business objectives of your organization. What are the values that will help further your objectives?
- Do you think you will be able to instil values at all levels of the organization just by introducing the policies?
- What have been the stated commitments of your organization towards the society and environment? Use a 'what-enables-it' analysis to arrive at the values that will strengthen your commitment in these two areas.
- In your organization, do you believe that there is uniform understanding of the values identified? What are the areas where there is ambiguity regarding how certain values are interpreted and applied?
- Given the pressures of periodic targets (quarterly, annual), there is a tendency to focus only on business issues that are connected with achieving the targets. In such a context, how will you identify opportunities for raising awareness about values?
- What are the top three areas where you find most values violations in your organization? What is the impact of these violations on the performance of the organization? What are the steps that can be taken to address these violations?

***

यद्यदाचरति श्रेष्ठः तत्तदेवेतरो जनः ।
स यत् प्रमाणं कुरुते लोकस्तदनुवर्तते ॥

Whatever the most excellent person practises, the other people
follow the same. That which he demonstrates by action, people
will follow that.

—Bhagavad Gita

WALKING THE TALK

> *I am afraid we must make the world honest before we can honestly say to our children that honesty is the best policy.*
>
> **—George Bernard Shaw**

Examine the given quote for just a minute. Doesn't it give a hint regarding what the responsibility of a leader should be?

Before we get into the subject of leadership, let us recapitulate the key points regarding values:

- Values are the substratum of vision, plan and strategy.
- Values are the foundations of every system, every function and every process.
- Values underline every decision at every level of the entire organization.
- Values have a positive impact on the bottom line.
- Values enhance creativity, innovation, productivity, quality and excellence.
- Values are the bedrock for a stress-free environment at work.
- Values are not just about fair accounting practices or preventing wrongdoing.
- Values go beyond honesty and integrity.
- Whenever we use words such as people and culture, we are, in essence, talking of values.

Values are not rules or a checklist of do's and don'ts.

Who is a Leader?

Leader and leadership are often quoted words in today's world, be it in a business context or otherwise. As with any of these terms, it makes sense to relook at the core purpose and meaning behind these words.

The answer to 'who is a leader' is 'the one who leads'. Very simple, isn't it.

If there is someone who leads, then two important obvious questions follow:

- Who or what is being led?
- What or where are they being led to? In other words, what goals are they being led to?

Who or What Is Being Led?

Would it be enough to say people—men and women—are being led? Is it a large number of human beings who are being led? Is it right to see them as herds? In the context of an organization, each individual is recruited for a specific purpose; he/she has a specific role and responsibility and he/she has come in because of something that he/she brings in to the organization's talent pool. In other words, each individual has an identity.

Then how can we say 'people are being led'. The moment we say people, we tend to see it en masse. It is individuals who are being led. Each individual has a unique identity, a unique personality.

When it comes to the subject of values, this distinction of seeing those being led as individuals makes all the difference. The individual with 'I' comes with his/her own mind and its nuances, that mind which is the seat of all values.

What or Where Are They Being Led To?

Perhaps most people don't think about this aspect of being a leader. Or for many this is to do with meeting the revenue targets of the organization or fulfilling the vision of the organization.

The true leader is concerned with both realizing the vision of the business and also ensuring that the employees are led to their success and well-being. This is as true for the head of a family as it is for the head of a large multinational corporation.

However, the reality is:

- *The Economic Times* shared that 46 per cent of the workforce in organizations in India suffers from some or other form of stress.
- Stress is leading to a higher risk of high BP and heart problems, obesity, diabetes, depression, gastrointestinal problems, accelerated aging and a host of other physical health problems.
- According to the World Health Organization, stress has become a worldwide epidemic.
- Pressure from workload, stringent deadlines and lack of managerial support are increasingly contributing to stress at the workplace.
- Health care costs resulting from stress at the workplace are on the rise across the world.

In short, we are seeing more stress and less well-being at the workplace. In such a scenario, it is for the leadership to lead the individuals in the organization to well-being.

Just by defining the leader as someone who motivates people to achieve the end goal(s), we are trivializing the role and its dimension.

A verse from an ancient text in India gives the etymology of the word *aachaarya* (spiritual guide or teacher). This very succinctly also captures the qualities of a leader from the point of view of values.

आचिनोति च शास्त्रार्थान् आचारे स्थापयत्यपि ।
स्वयमाचरते यस्मात् तस्मादाचार्य उच्यते ॥
—Apasthamba Dharmasutra

One who gathers or acquires knowledge from the purport of the scriptures, instils them in one's conduct and behaviour and behaves or conducts oneself accordingly is called an *aachaarya*.

These are words which directly apply to the leadership of any organization which wishes to create and sustain a values-based organization. The focus is entirely on demonstration of values through one's conduct, that is, decisions and actions.

An example of walking the talk was shared by a senior consultant at a leading consulting organization in the energy sector. He said that compliance to stated values was very obvious in his organization, and that was the basic norm.

I worked more than 15 years in this organization and have an insider's view on the adherence to values. One reason I think I remained there for so long has been the quality of work I was doing as well as the work culture. Our organization did take values very seriously. The core values had been very clearly articulated. We had frequent sessions—at least twice a year—wherein values, especially to do with integrity and ethics in business, were discussed, and current and fresh examples of violations and their consequences were shared.

What influenced me was walking the talk. There were examples of senior people in the hierarchy being severely punished—even let go—for violations of values. One example was that of a senior leader in the organization who was influencing a customer stakeholder improperly. There was another where there was a value infringement in a procurement decision. In both cases, the action was taken swiftly.

Whenever values were not being upheld, there were conse-quences, and management was transparent and quick about it. I remember feeling good every time I heard of such instances. I felt that it wasn't just talk and I felt a closer connection to the organization having the feeling that I work for one where we consciously do the right thing and not get tempted and violate values as I knew some competitors were doing.

Qualities of a Values-Based Leader: An Example

When asked, 'what aspects of the senior leadership have helped the organization cultivate a culture of values in the organization', a senior executive from a large corporation in the transportation sector had the following to say:

- Inspiring leadership
- Fearless and bold in taking decisions and standing by them
- Trust in people

She further added, the senior leadership because of its conduct and style of management inculcated the following in the employees:

- Courage to face different external agencies
- Tolerance to allow others to learn from mistakes that was reinforced by trusting the employees in their actions over a period of time
- Freedom to take decisions in their sphere of work (that would help them address the necessary challenges in the field)
- Values in dealing with contractors; this was reinforced by the motto—contractors' success means our success
- A mindset of service before self

Rising above Policies and Rules

There are instances when we are in a tight spot and we approach a senior executive in the organization seeking a redress. Instead of getting a solution, we are shown the rule book. We know how frustrating this can be. Values-based leadership transcends rules and policies. The following anecdote shared by a young executive in the health care sector illustrates this point:

We were in the initial stages of our growth. Because of the nature of circumstances then, some of us often used to end up working on holidays or over weekends. One day, I approached the COO of the organization to check if I could take a compensatory day off because I had been working the last couple of weekends. He said, 'No, we don't have such a policy'.

He went on to add, 'However, let your boss know and you just take the day off one of these days'.

This demonstration of integrity, fairness and empathy on the part of the COO was an important lesson for me, where I learnt to take decisions to help others even though it was not in conformance with company policies.

Values-Based Leadership Mindset

Here, in this context we are not talking of just leadership, but values-based leadership. What is significant regarding this leader is:

- The leader espouses values and lives the values
- The leader also inspires others to live the values by being a role model

Given this backdrop, what are the changes required in the mindset and approach to become a values-based leader?

- *Self-centred to other-centred:* The focus shifts from oneself, one's achievements, one's goals, etc., to the individuals around. The organization's success and the individuals' success become the key concern.

- *Target of profits to vision of well-being:* Not that revenue, profits and growth of the organization are not important, but all that follows the overarching vision of well-being of the employees of the organization.

- *Leading people to inspiring individuals:* The leader sees people not en masse but as individuals, each with his or her own unique personality, aspirations and capabilities. When the focus is the well-being of individuals, seeing people en masse will not serve the purpose.

  Linda A. Hill, Professor of Business Administration at the Harvard Business School, says: 'Leadership is about making emotional connections to motivate and inspire people, and our effectiveness at doing this has strong cultural overtones'. She further adds, 'You have to create an environment in which they are engaged and in which the collective talent of team members is tapped by having everyone take the lead at some point'.

This idea of making emotional connections can happen only when the leader begins to shift the focus from people en mass to individuals.

- *Systems and processes to foundation of values:* While systems and processes will continue to be there, the foundation of it all will be values. A value-based culture will naturally facilitate better interpretation of processes and a more effective application.

- *Facilitate collaboration in teams to facilitate collaboration of minds:* One of the most significant benefits of a values-based culture is collaboration leading to individuals realizing their true potential. This can be realized only when we see collaboration at the level of the mind, rather than at the gross level of people.

An organization might get the best of individuals in various fields, but to ensure that their collective output is substantially more than the sum of the individual outputs, the leader has to facilitate collaboration of minds and intelligences. It is not enough to see them as a team.

- *Decisions taken at the top level to making every manager an inspired decision-maker:* Everyone in the organization sees decisions being taken at the top and then rolled down, but a value-based leader creates a culture where the power of values and the inspired environment it creates transforms every manager into an inspired decision-maker.

Key Attributes of a Values-Based Leader

Whenever we talk of any particular quality of a human, that quality by itself sometimes seems to feel incomplete or perhaps needs to be qualified. For example, when you talk of kindness, some may feel that it seems like a soft trait, particularly in the context of a business environment. However, saying 'he is kind, but firm' conveys a different feeling.

Based on our study of having examined successful leaders in business organizations, we drew up a list of five traits that form the core of a value-based leader. We felt these traits are the most significant which set apart a true leader.

- *Humility with courage:* In the article 'Humility Key to Effective Leadership', Jacqueline Ghosen writes: 'A follow-up study that is forthcoming in Organization Science using data from more than 700 employees and 218 leaders confirmed that leader humility is associated with more learning-oriented teams, more engaged employees and lower voluntary employee turnover'. The importance of humility cannot be overemphasized. Some have a misconception that the quality of humility has a tone of weakness to it. Actually it takes strength and courage to be humble. Being humble, the leader:
  - o Is open to points of view coming from any direction and from anyone.
  - o Is accepting any situation that arises.
  - o Respects every human being for who he/she is.

  Jim Collins, in his book *Good to Great*, said this of what he calls Level 5 leaders: 'Self-effacing, quiet, reserved, even shy—these leaders are a paradoxical blend of personal humility and professional will. They are more like Lincoln and Socrates than Patton or Caesar'.

- *Empathy with impersonality:* To be an inspiring leader, an effective facilitator of employee development, a good coach and a dynamic team player, the first quality that every successful leader thinks about is empathy. In the context of the quality of being empathetic, it is very crucial that the individual is unbiased, impersonal.

  Findings shared by the Centre for Creative Leadership reveal that 'empathy is positively related to job performance. Managers who show more empathy toward direct reports are viewed as better performers in their job by their bosses'.

- *Vision with foresight:* The prudence or ability of looking forward, even when you have a clear vision statement for the organization, is essential for the leader to be able to inspire individuals to become inspired employees.

The founders of Sony had stated the following as part of the founding prospectus: 'The first and primary motive for setting up this company was to create a stable work environment where engineers who had a deep and profound appreciation for technology could realize their societal mission and work to their heart's content'.

- *Adaptability with integrity:* Adaptability refers not only to adapting oneself to changing industry trends, changing technology trends, changing user expectations, changing economic conditions, etc., but also to be able to adapt to peoples' changing needs and expectations.

Responding to changes around—be it in circumstances or in people—calls for an integrated personality. Integrity offers that stable substratum to decisions and actions, even under changing circumstances.

Charles Darwin said, 'It is not the strongest of the species that survives, nor the most intelligent. It is the one that is most adaptable to change'. A value-based leader complements adaptability with integrity which facilitates the process of acceptance and adoption by others more facile.

Integrity is the cornerstone to transparency. Value-based organizations naturally lend themselves to good governance.

Infosys founder N. R. Narayana Murthy said the following about good governance:

Good governance is about doing what is fair in a transparent manner with full accountability accepted by senior leaders and board members for their actions. Good governance results from following the adages—when in doubt, disclose; and let the good news take the stairs and let the bad news take the elevator.

- *Compassion with firmness:* Compassion is a sense of deep sympathy for another accompanied by a strong desire to alleviate the suffering. For a leader, who always strives for the well-being of the individuals he/she leads, compassion becomes essential. When compassion is accompanied by firmness, the leader carries a certain poise and stability in all interactions, decisions and actions.

Most challenging decisions and actions on the part of the organization, namely lay-offs, punishments for values violations, dealing with customer grievances and termination of contracts require leaders to have a compassionate outlook so that the heartburns and bitterness in relationships can be avoided, and the matters can be settled amicably.

Leaders Nurture Values-Based Culture

The whole purview of values being very subtle and nebulous, everything depends on the ability of the leadership of the organization to envision, instil and sustain a value-based culture in the organization.

In the famous Iceberg model for competencies, while skills and knowledge form one-ninth of its volume (above water), values form a critical part of the rest which lie beneath the surface. Leaders need to recognize this truth and play a leading role in the context of values by being role models for value-based decisions, conduct and actions.

Here, we examine some critical areas from the values-based leader's point of view.

Live the values

Values are about what we really aspire to be and live by, and not only how we want to be perceived. Offering only lip service to values, without living them, particularly when it comes to leaders and managers, will lead to conflict in the minds of others. Repeated instances of conflict will eventually lead to disbelief regarding values.

A senior manager in a manufacturing organization based in Europe shared the following experience:

> I had been chosen for the ultimate award in our organization in recognition of my continued performance over the last five years. I had been invited to a very exotic location to join an elite team in the organization for a weekend. During the awards ceremony, the head of the organization spoke, and there were lot of references to integrity, empathy, values, trust and commitment. I was watching all this in stunned silence. In the last many years in this organization, I had never heard of these terms in the organization, let alone experience these in the workplace.

> This episode left me wondering if this is what values are all about, something to be spoken about during such events, meant to motivate others in the organization. Subsequent to the event too, I never heard about these terms from the management. Overall, it left me with a bitter taste about the subject of values.

The most important point to note is that such deep impressions in employees, resulting from repeated experiences, are very detrimental to the culture of the organization and in some cases almost impossible to repair. We met some who have superannuated, who still carry strong negative views regarding values in the context of businesses.

The following quote from William S. Burroughs is as much relevant to values as it is to quality: 'You can't fake quality any more than you can fake a good meal'.

It is not enough to be seen as values oriented. The true benefits of value orientation will accrue only when the intent is genuine. I am sure everyone can find enough examples in his/her family life to illustrate this point.

One simple way to talk of values, to communicate values and to instruct employees about values is to live the values. Leaders, through their conduct, also inspire other managers to set an example for teams to emulate.

In December 2014, when an AirAsia plane with 162 passengers disappeared near Indonesia, the Chief Executive Tony Fernandes immediately rushed to the point of departure and was in touch with the families of the passengers and crew. This quick act of concern and compassion from the head of the airlines was appreciated by the analysts, and the airlines received favourable reviews. However, what matters in the long run is the genuineness and integrity of the leaders in dealing with such situations.

Reacting to that act of the chief executive, head of research at an investment bank in Malaysia said in a statement, 'I think the main thing right now is to protect their brand, and I think that will be instrumental in the future of their company'.

If a leader responds to such situations with the only thought of saving the brand, how would you react to that?

Integrity is the key

This anecdote shared by a CEO of an FMCG multinational corporation demonstrates how integrity is the very core to many of the decisions in the organization, and any violations of that has adverse impact on those around.

I was head of a business unit at that time and was reporting to the Country Head. He was known to be ambitious to a fault and was clearly looking for fast career growth in the larger organization. Our organization was an old and respected one and was known for its values. One of the values we had was to ensure everyone benefited in the value chain including our distributors. Early on in his tenure, my boss asked me to push unrequired inventories to the distributors (to show increase in quarterly sales). When I pushed back, his response was that I was not a team player and we had frequent arguments over this issue.

This period was both good and bad for me. It was stressful to go to work, knowing each day would have an unpleasant encounter. I also knew people under me respected me a lot for doing the right thing and they knew what was happening.

Looking back, this period strengthened me as a leader and I would like to attribute my long-term success to such learning moments. The upholding of the values in the end depends on the individual.

Here, the Country Head gave more importance to his business goals while compromising on the interest of customers and distributors who are very integral to the business ecosystem of the organization.

While integrity at the level of each individual is important, it is also essential that integrity of speech, decisions and actions is maintained across all aspects of the organization's conduct. In other words, you cannot let the decision or action in one part of the organization contradict the decision or action in another section.

Values are dependent on each other, you cannot violate certain values and expect certain other values to be upheld.

Let us examine the following scenario: In trying to be austere in the realm of costs, an organization spends enormous amount on consultancy costs for over six months and takes a decision to lay off a large number of people and one fine day announces the decision without any advance warning or indication. How would you interpret this action?

Across the organization, conflicts like the one in the aforementioned scenario, at times, present themselves in our individual context too.

Hui Chen, a compliance expert in the Justice Department's (USA) Fraud Section, resigned in 2017 and had this to say, 'I am not willing nor able to compartmentalize my values as an [ethics and compliance] professional, a citizen, and a human being'. Even if we don't know the context and the circumstances that led to her resignation, what she has said is very significant.

In simple words, one cannot live values partially, cannot switch off values at home and switch them on at work.

Sustaining Values in a Constantly Changing Human Resource Pool

The culture of values is held and sustained by people. The work environment, however, is constantly undergoing a churn.

The following are the challenges:

- As the organization grows in size, in terms of human resources, how do you keep the values alive? Newer employees are always joining the organization. How to instil values in these new recruits and integrate them into the values culture of the existing employees?
- It has been observed that as an organization grows in size, people or new businesses, there is a tendency to undergo some dilution in values. How to prevent this?
- How do you integrate personalities—old and new, senior and junior, experienced and inexperienced, contrasting functional responsibilities, etc.?

Our intent here is to only point to the potential concerns. The solution to these will depend on the organization's culture, quality of leadership and values penetration within the organization.

In 'Why Good People Sometimes Do Bad Things? 52 Reflections on Ethics at Work', Muel Kaptein (2012) describes the following problem:

> Corruption is not purely a question of rotten apples (contaminated or infected individuals). The barrel, or even the orchard, could be contaminated and spoil the apples. Corruption can be ingrained in the environment so that in the end everyone is infected with it. Just as humidity influences the extent of rot in the apples, the air quality in an organization (the organizational culture) influences the extent of corruption among employees, because employees are continually breathing this air in (and back out again).

> It is important to examine what factors help and hinder the rotting process. We must also ask who is behind the barrels and the orchard. Who are the owners, growers and pickers? Often these people remain out of range when

scandals erupt. Furthermore it is important to establish who and what determine the quality of the apples. A fruit grower's task is not only to prevent rotting, but to cultivate apples of a high quality. In organizations, it is therefore not so much a matter of preventing employees from becoming corrupt as ensuring that they flourish and bear fruit.

Values-based leaders are able to address this crucial point of 'how to cultivate apples of high quality'.

Grooming the Next Level for Values-Based Leadership

One of the challenges always faced by leaders is the task of grooming the next level managers to move into the responsibility of values-based leadership. This grooming and nurturing of the next level is also one of the main channels through which the culture of values-based management and value-based work environment can be furthered.

Being Able to Feel Subtle Values Violations

Most organizations see violations only when they hit the business of the organizations hard. They keep ignoring the subtle signals and are not able to see the long-term impact of those, until they snowball into something huge, which then calls for dedicated effort, resources and costs.

Sometimes managers become insensitive to violations in the workplace and simply allow them to become such a transparent part of the culture that people begin to see them as a way of life.

Mark of values-based leadership is in being able to sense the subtle values violations and prevent them from becoming gross violations.

Sustainability of a Business Organization

When we refer to the word sustainability, most people believe that it includes the notion of sustainability of the universe and its natural resources. However, here we are simply referring to the sustainability of the business and the organization itself.

According to Mark Goodburn, the Global Head of Advisory, KPMG International, 'The average life span of today's multinational, Fortune 500-size corporation is 40 to 50 years'. He goes on to add that 'almost 50% of the Fortune 500 from 1999 had disappeared from the list just ten years later'. According to another study by scientists at the Santa Fe Institute in New Mexico, businesses generally survive for about 10 years.

These statistics do present a dismal picture for all businesses in the years to come. However, here we would like to present a line of thinking which is worth exploring for long-term sustenance of a business organization.

There are about 1,000 businesses founded before the year 1700 that are still standing tall today. What is also amazing is that more than half of these businesses are based in Japan. What makes Japan unique in this? Most of Japan's oldest companies are family-run businesses.

What is that one factor that helps family-run businesses sustain for long term? It is no surprise that that one factor is trust. In order to sustain this trust, two values these family-run businesses have relied on are as follows:

- Communicate openly and honestly
- Be fair and be seen as fair

A Country Head, India, of a leading social-sector firm shared the following experience with the organization's CEO, which underlined the importance of openness:

We are growing as a firm and are going through a rather interesting period, trying out many new initiatives. Every year, when our goal setting and performance appraisal process starts, it starts at the top. This year too, the CEO met with all executives reporting to him, during which he shared his goals for the year and asked each one of us for feedback on his performance (last year) and any other feedback for him to become more effective. The meeting was unhurried.

I found the meeting energizing. It connected us even closer as a team, and more importantly with our leader. Our organization gives importance to personal connect and collaboration. I experienced it first-hand in such instances and I try to do the same with my teams. Such occasions also reinforced my belief in values such as openness, involving others, sharing one's own personal goals and plans, seeking feedback in such an open forum.

Such a demonstration of openness, camaraderie and role modelling, while guiding and coaching senior executives, also removes any threat from transparency and provides psychological safety.

Arie P. de Geus, who was the head of Shell Oil Company's Strategic Planning Group, in his book *The Living Company* says, 'Companies die because their managers focus on the economic activity of producing goods and services, and they forget that their organizations' true nature is that of a community of humans'.

And when we realize that the organization is a community of humans, we can't ignore the fact that what animates and activates that community is values.

Values Dialogues

Sanjay: There are many occasions when I find that the members of the senior management team act in a manner which goes against the core values identified by our organization. That has been creating a lot of stress in me. In such a situation, how do I advocate values in my team composed of junior team members?

Sheela: I think this is perhaps the most serious situation an organization can face when the senior management of an organization is perceived as not upholding the very values it has chosen for the organization. This also becomes a very difficult situation to recover from.

Sanjay: Are you suggesting that nothing can be done about it? Are we to just accept this situation as the end of the road?

Sheela: I am not hinting at that. Let us discuss this situation and explore it in some detail. When you say senior management, who are you referring to? Does it include the CEO and the entire top team? If you say that the entire team is in violation of values, it is then a tough road ahead. This is very rarely the case. Please elaborate.

Sanjay: When I said the senior management team, I am not including everyone in this. There are a couple of them. But they are very visible ones.

Sheela: Are any of them the founders of the organization? Because if the founders themselves are in violation, then it becomes even more difficult and employees across the organization lose faith in the system.

Sanjay: No, they are not the founders.

Sheela: Organizations which have embarked on the journey of values often have put in place a system to handle grievances of employees. Employees can take recourse to that. It of course depends on the nature of the violations you are concerned with. Organizations which are sincere about their intent for having a values-based culture may also have some senior person who could be approached with this grievance.

Sanjay: I get the general idea about that. But how do I instil values in my own team?

Sheela: Here is what I would suggest. Depending on the prevailing culture, different managers may approach the problem differently. Needless to say, there is no one way of addressing such issues. From your question, I gather that you are particular about creating a culture of values within your team. Since you are clear about that, separate that issue at the top from the context of your team. I know it is easier said than done. This is because, as long as you have a team and a project or task at hand, your first concern is to accomplish that task and to accomplish it well. As a manager, it is also your responsibility to act as a shield between your team and the concerns in other parts of the organization.

Sanjay: That's tough.

Sheela: I know it is not easy. It is not impossible either. Otherwise, if you let the team be influenced by what's going on outside and that lowers the morale in the team, it can adversely impact the outcome of the project. And the first step towards that is to be clear that you will first focus on your team and project first and worry about all else later.

Sanjay: Thank you. Though I don't have all the answers I need, it gives me some ideas to make a beginning.

Values Reflection

Introspect and deliberate upon these questions, as you go forward in strengthening your organization's culture of values:

- When values violations go beyond a threshold value, they may become a crime. What are your observations regarding this statement?
- When you look at yourself as an individual, why do some people have a long-term relationship with you? That's perhaps the core of who you are. What's the equivalent of the same in the case of your organization?
- What do your customers and vendors value in you today? What do you value in them? Are all the elements just relating to revenue and costs?
- Your organization has taken recourse to lay-off as a major cost-cutting drive. As a manager, you have been asked to identify a list of members in your team who would be asked to resign. How would you approach this challenge of identifying the team members? What other measures would you like to take to ensure that the setback to the individuals can be mitigated?
- In the context of the leadership qualities discussed in this chapter, how would you rate yourself on the various qualities?
- On the aspect of living the values, how would you assess yourself? Which are the areas where you need to strengthen yourself in this regard?

* * *

आपदि मित्र परीक्षा शूरपरीक्षा च रणाङ्गणे ।
विनये वंश परीक्षा च शील परीक्षा तु धनक्षये ॥

A friend's test is in adversity; the test of a valiant one is on the battlefield; the test of a family is in its humility and the test of one's character is in loss of wealth.

—Subhaashitam

PERSONAL JOURNEY

> *The trite saying that honesty is the best policy has met with the just criticism that honesty is not policy. The real honest man is honest from conviction of what is right, not from policy.*
>
> —**Robert E. Lee**

While the subject of discussion in this book has been values in the context of the organization, the primary seat of values is the individual. When we talk of values in teams or organization, remember that the values subsist in the individual, not in the team or organization. Since both teams and organizations are made up of individuals, we refer to values in the context of teams and organizations.

The focus of this chapter is entirely on the individual, because it is he/she who has to embody those values.

What Identifies the Individual?

Let us examine an item everyone is familiar with—a curriculum vitae. It offers a glimpse of an individual's education, career and some other personal information. From the organization's point of view, this is the starting point for taking a decision regarding recruitment of the individual into the organization.

While the resume gives an idea of what you have done so far, it does not provide adequate information about who you are. The important point to note is that the decision to recruit you is not entirely based on what you have done, but primarily on who you are or what kind of personality you have and what you are capable of in the future. In fact, much of the discussions during the recruitment process revolve around your personality or, at least, the recruitment team is constantly trying to figure out, who you are as a person. Even the various tests are aimed at figuring out that—your character, interactional ability, managerial and leadership qualities, etc. When a founder of one of the leading IT organizations recruited the CEO, the founder remarked that the CEO candidate was finally hired for his high learnability index.

What is it that defines your personality? What are the constituents of your personality?

When someone asks you what defines your personality, you would perhaps talk about certain qualities and attributes of your personality. You would, for example, describe yourself as a person of integrity, an open-minded, hard-working, patient individual, etc. What are these qualities or traits? These are nothing but values—values you cherish and values you have upheld all your life.

Ask yourself the following questions: How do you evaluate a person? What makes you connect with a person? What makes you like a person or otherwise? The answer is the same: the values the individual espouses.

Values define the individual! Values identify the individual!

Certain values are more prominently noticed by others; hence, you hear statements like 'he is an honest person', 'she is a compassionate lady', and so on.

Fundamentally, All Are Values Oriented

An important point to note is that every individual adheres to a set of values, which he/she has consciously chosen or subconsciously imbibed. But we do differ in our values orientation. What varies is the degree to which different values are upheld. So to say that a particular individual is not values oriented will not be an accurate statement.

Another point to remember is that while we may be generally truthful in our behaviour, but in a certain instance, during a particular interaction, we may have acted in an untruthful way.

Here is something else that is quite commonly observed in the workplace. Young executives who have just joined an organization, for some of whom it is the first job, put in long hours to ensure that they complete the tasks they have been assigned to on time. Where did they get this commitment from?

Let us realize that it is in all of us to act in a manner that is values oriented. Organizations should recognize this fundamental point.

What we need to introspect over are the following:

- How to sustain those commitment levels that new recruits exhibited?
- Over time why and how did that commitment come down?
- What is the cause of that change?

Instilling Values

Let us begin with a quote from Aristotle that brings another dimension to the idea of value or virtue:

> Excellence is an art won by training and habituation. We do not act rightly because we have virtue or excellence, but we rather have those because we have acted rightly. We are what we repeatedly do. Excellence, then, is not an act but a habit.

The family and the context of the family is the first school, when it comes to values. Of course, when we say 'family', we are referring to the members of the family. We imbibe the values prevalent in the family just like that. There are no classes held. There are no lessons. There is no homework. There are no exams. We simply learn by being in that environment.

As we begin our interactions in school, with friends and society, etc., these values start guiding us. We perhaps begin to notice what we stand for. But values are still in the background. We most often are not conscious of these values and may not think about what values to inculcate or what traits to discard.

Our exposure to the school environment is the first arena outside of the family. This also has a significant impact on who we are and what we become, not only in terms of which profession but also in terms of our personality and character.

All through these years, we soak in things through a process of osmosis—a completely invisible process and an involuntary process. All the experiences shape us and our personality.

When we enter our first job, we enter a new kind of environment, with which our association continues for a significant part of the rest of our lives. It is almost as if we have a new set of rules to life and living.

Our interactions are of a different kind, and the rules and principles governing these interactions seem different from the ones we have been used to so far. But like the book *All I Really Need to Know I Learned in Kindergarten* by Robert Fulghum says, in reality the principles are very much the same as we had in our childhood.

My Own Values versus the Organization's Values

Let us begin this discussion by examining this experience shared by a young executive in an IT services organization. He then had just about a year's experience in the industry.

> We were working on a project where we had to submit our time sheets at the end of every week. The client was then billed based on those time sheets. One day, the account manager came up to me and asked me to fudge some time sheets. For someone so young and inexperienced with the ways of the corporate world, this came as a great shock. But my own values acquired through my upbringing came to my rescue. I simply refused to do that, though I was a little apprehensive. The account manager was obviously not very pleased with me. He tried to justify his request; however, I stuck to my position. Later, I went and reported the matter to the CEO (being a small organization, we had easy access to the CEO) and HR. To my surprise, there

was no reaction or action from either. With the head of the organization showing no concern or urgency regarding my complaint, it was no surprise that the account manager or HR reacted the way they did. Having spent another six months or so in that organization, I left them.

Such a demonstration of lack of integrity at different levels in the organization certainly has a deep impact on us, and particularly when it happens early on in our career.

We all have our own set of values. Some use terms like value system, principles, etc. Through some very subtle and subconscious processes, we find that we have imbibed certain values which guide us through life and its interactions. Quite often, most of us are exposed to these, when someone (either during our education or at work) asks us to articulate our values. One favourite interview question used by an executive is: What are the top three values you cherish? Apart from these circumstances, sometimes a challenging experience in our life might trigger this question in us. Irrespective of whether we have reflected and articulated or not, each one of us lives by some values.

'The secret of my success in one word is Integrity', says Dr E. Sreedharan, the former managing director of the Delhi Metro Rail Corporation.

When we enter the work environment, we are faced with a new challenge. Our own values, which have been shaped since childhood, are confronted with another set of values that this new environment at the workplace stands for. It is a significant time in the lives of most of us.

If we examine carefully, we have faced this kind of situation earlier too, through our years in school, college, university, etc., but this experience at the workplace is strikingly different.

It is not that the organization's values are opposed to our own values. What often happens is that the value we give importance to as an individual is not high on the list of priorities for the organization. For example, Rakesh as an individual may hold kindness and compassion as the most important values, but the organization he works for—a manufacturing unit—may not even list these as part of its core values. This does not mean that kindness and compassion are not important in the workplace; just that there are other values which are much more crucial from this organization's point of view. This need not be seen as a conflict.

Conflict comes in when the values we hold dear in our life are violated at the organizational level. For example, if Rakesh finds that in a certain situation, the organization dealt with an employee in a very unkind and harsh manner when Rakesh felt that all the employee needed was tenderness and compassion.

Let us examine the following quote by Swami Vivekananda in *Karma Yoga: The Yoga of Action*:

> If you really want to judge the character of a man, look not at his great performances. Every fool may become a hero at one time or another. Watch a man do his most common actions; those are indeed the things which will tell you the real character of a great man. Great occasions rouse even the lowest of human beings to some kind of greatness, but he alone is the really great man whose character is great always, the same wherever he be.

Source: https://www.vivekananda.net/PDFBooks/KarmaYoga. pdf (accessed on 28 March 2019)

Whether we are at home or at work, whether it is part of the organization's policy or not, whether we are under the supervision of someone or not, our actions are governed by the same set of values we hold very dear to us. And those values come through in the most mundane activities. You might have come across individuals who demonstrate the same values of fairness, kindness, empathy, etc., whether they are in the company of the junior level employees, or they are interacting with the bosses in the boardroom.

If at all, the organization's values add another dimension to our own set of values, because they are essential in the context of the business. It is unlikely that the organization's values will be in contradiction to your own personal values that you have cherished from childhood.

Values Conflicts Strengthen Us

The path of values is not one of fun. There is a lot of strain involved. Value-based conduct always challenges you every moment. It is not, to use the cliché, a bed of roses, by any stretch of imagination. There is obviously a greater reason for people resorting to value-based living. At one level, it is quite elementary. Values are what sustain society. The following statement from the Manusmriti reinforces this point:

धर्मो रक्षति रक्षितः

Dharma protects those who protect dharma.

If we were to present this in terms of the 'values': Values protect those who uphold values.

Your values are tested quite often at the workplace. Some draw your attention more than others. For example, there would have been many instances when you would have arrived at a meeting before or on time and waited for quite a few minutes before others sauntered in. You feel that it is almost the culture of the organization to begin meetings late. You, however, do not take these violations too seriously, although it is frustrating at times.

On the other hand, there are violations that impact you deeply. There are episodes we have come across at the end of which individuals have chosen to leave the organization because of the violations in values.

Conflicts and friction associated with upholding values strengthen us and also our conviction regarding our values. The quote by Rabindranath Tagore further illustrates this point:

> The sword of dharma rubbed on the stone of *adharma* became sharp.

At the same time, during our research, we came across a few individuals whose experiences relating to values at the workplace have completely turned them away from values. These individuals are very cynical and believe that values do not have a place in business organizations.

One senior executive who was part of a leading FMCG company had this to say:

> I have never seen organizations uphold values; I have seen very few individuals uphold them at their own level. But it is more because of their own personal values. For me, at the organizational level, when it comes to business and numbers, values take a back seat. The larger picture is—the corporate world is not capable of upholding values, because of their structure and competition. And for this very reason, I quit the corporate world.

For this executive, personal experiences over the years working through various organizations had reinforced this belief. He, however, added, 'At the same time, I have met some very wonderful people during my time with business organizations, who have been exemplary in upholding values. But they have been a rarity, and they were almost an island by themselves in the vast ocean called business'.

This is an example of how one's experience shapes his/her thinking and belief systems.

In various discussions we held with corporate executives (at different levels in the organizational hierarchy), they were increasingly sure that every time they were able to stand by their values, it reinforced their conviction in their own values. At the same time, every time there were conflicts in the mind—when the personal values were in conflict with the action or behaviour of some at the workplace—it made the individual deeply introspect over the situation.

This conscious introspection or the internal tussle with the outside contradiction often provides answers which reinforce our stance on the values we cherish.

Another important point to keep in mind is that our perspective regarding the situations and the assessment of those situations seem to change in some of the cases. This is what a young executive shared with us, who was then part of a business process outsourcing organization:

> In a particular project I was a part of, we were cruising comfortably towards achieving our deadline. Suddenly, there was some change to the end date, and we found that we were in a crisis mode. We were having to work extra hours, and it was causing a lot of stress in all of us. I felt that the management, who otherwise talks of values, had violated many of those values they talk about. But as I grew in experience and started moving up the organizational hierarchy, I realized that on certain occasions, decisions like changing deadlines do happen and it is not necessarily because of values violations. In fact in one such scenario, we catered to a request from a long-term client, because it was a crisis situation for that client because of a commitment they had made to one of their clients; and we were merely helping them, for no additional financial gains for us.

Such instances do change our perspective regarding situations. We begin to understand that, sometimes, what appears to be violation of values for one perceiver might actually be upholding values to another.

Guidelines for individuals

- Values-based individuals face many challenges and hurdles. This is because when the surrounding environment is not values based, there is bound to be friction, many obstacles and challenges. Remember your physics lesson: 'friction is a part of motion'.
- Our values come to the light and are put to test whenever we are faced with decision points. What decisions we make and how we act determine our value system.
- Values are not driven by returns on investment or cost–benefit analysis. Every time we cannot do a cost–benefit analysis before we decide to act in a values-oriented manner.
- Values-oriented behaviour has to be a natural response. It is not an action that is a result of analysis. This intent is

beautifully articulated by the following quote, 'Honesty is the best policy, but he who acts on that principle is not an honest person' (source unknown).

- You do not need any inspiration to be values based; it is the fundamental nature of a human being.
- At the level of teams too, we need values to support each other, guide each other and stand by each other.
- The reward for being values oriented is the enrichment you gain from it.
- It is not that those who violate values do not have choices to make; they are also faced with tough decisions. What matters is how and in what favour you decide.

What facilitates values-based living (among employees)?

- Conviction in values
- Support of peers, seniors and subordinates
- Respect for others
- Ability to see violations even when they were not obvious
- Fearless about consequences of value adherence

Each employee has to take the lead

Often, as individuals, we find it hard to adhere to values, because we don't find many instances of others practising them. Let us take the example of driving. Particularly in India, we find some crossings are notorious. No one seems to stop at the red signal. Everyone drives on as if they are on green.

However, you may have encountered the following situation: When you stop, every one stops seeing you. Have you wondered what this indicates?

There are many out there who want someone else to lead and show the way. You might have noticed this in the context of a team too. Often, if there is one person in the group who favours the right, the group tends to move towards that. We are not saying that this is always the case. But it is definitely so among reasonable individuals.

A few conscientious individuals can make a big difference.

Togetherness Is Strength

An observation we have heard in quite a few of our discussions is: 'After all I am an individual. There are so many negative forces. In the final analysis, it almost doesn't matter whether I uphold values or not'.

At the same time, there are those who realize their own role in contributing to the organization's values even if they are alone in this endeavour. Of course, there are those who are very indifferent to the subject.

Let us begin at the level of the immediate team we belong to. We are never (almost never) alone. We have a group of individuals who are part of the same shared objective and purpose, which is the team's common goal. In such a scenario, the strength of the team comes from the strength provided by the presence of each of the individuals.

In such a scenario, if you examine carefully, what matters is to understand that we all share a common goal. That goal is our common identity. Once we have that feeling of identity, then naturally the values associated with teamwork and collaboration kick in. Once we believe that the entire team is there together, it provides us additional courage and support to stand by what we believe in.

When we are facing a situation alone, sometimes we may not have the courage to stand up to an unjust action or an unfair stance. But when we realize that we are not alone and are part of the team, it lends us the necessary courage to stand up and face the situation according to our own value system or organizational values, depending on the context.

Unstated Values

When we visit the websites of various organizations and examine their values, we come across the same or similar words in many places—integrity, compassion, empathy, fairness, teamwork, truthfulness, transparency and so on. Of course, organizations do clarify the meaning and relevance of the values in their contexts.

An organization ends up stating only those values that in its view contribute the most to its culture and facilitate its success. This does not mean that these are the only values or that the others are not important. There are those values that all are expected to uphold, for example, honesty.

Sakichi Toyoda, the founder of Toyota, had the following five main principles that guided him:

- Always be faithful to your duties, thereby contributing to the company and to the overall good.
- Always be studious and creative, striving to stay ahead of the times.
- Always be practical and avoid frivolousness.
- Always strive to build a home-like atmosphere at work that is warm and friendly.
- Always have respect for spiritual matters, and remember to be grateful at all times.

Let us take a look at some of the values which some organizations have as their stated values; interestingly, these are not spelt out in just one word but written as phrases:

- Taking responsibility for what we do
- Respecting others' point of view and belief systems
- Refraining from constant fault-finding with others or the organization
- Being open in offering feedback during meetings
- Accepting others as they are
- Not blaming others and forgiving others' mistakes
- Treating all co-workers, customers, vendors and all other stakeholders with respect
- Be committed to the team's and organization's goals
- Trust others in the team and in the organization
- Be loyal to the goals of the team and organization
- Be ready to support others in the organization
- Acknowledge the participation of others in the team
- Be open to take feedback from others around

Each one of these has been identified by the organizations as essential for their success.

Responsibility of the Manager

While each employee in the organization has equal responsibility towards upholding the values of the organization, the managers have some additional responsibilities in the context of sustaining the culture of values. Following are some of the very important points expected of the managers at the various levels in the organization in relation to facilitating the culture of values:

- Create an environment which is conducive to upholding of values
- Create an atmosphere where people are able to uphold values without any fear or threats from opposing forces
- Provide necessary training to all employees to help them understand the values the organization stands for
- Stand by and support the employees in difficult situations so that they feel empowered and encouraged to stand by the values, particularly in challenging situations
- Be sensitive to values violations in the organization, however minor they may be perceived to be
- Dwell on the circumstances and conditions that lead to values violations
- Regularly seek feedback from employees in order to understand instances of violations that you have not been able to sense
- While upholding a value is important, one should also be seen as upholding the value. For example, it is important to be fair, but it is also important to be seen as being fair.
- Trust others: It is not enough to say 'trust me'. The relationship of trust begins with trusting the other; thereafter, comes a stage when you are in a position to say 'trust me' and the other person will trust you.

The following episode shared by a Head of Finance of a KPO organization of a consulting company tells us how management with empathy can go a long way in strengthening trust between management and employees:

Our office was based in India and the parent company was in New York. I joined the place a few years after it had been operational. My role was to streamline all finance-related processes. I started liking the culture of our organization as I felt the senior team was open to new ideas and respected everyone. This feeling further got strengthened when I noticed some non-compliance issues in the way financial postings were being made prior to my joining, by my predecessor who was no longer in the firm. According to me, correcting the prior errors and putting in place a new process would initially cost the organization a fairly large amount (which was not planned for). I was initially hesitant in broaching this topic but seeing the receptiveness of the CEO of our local office, I felt encouraged to present the problem and solution in as clear terms as possible. The CEO was fully supportive and along with me worked on the plan to convince the international parent office to immediately execute the suggestions. I knew that there would be some reflection on the CEO for letting it happen in his watch. My respect for the CEO grew post this incident. I remember feeling an enhanced respect for him and was energized to fully contribute to the process changes he wanted. One reason I stayed there for more than 8 years was the CEO.

By demonstrating empathy, listening, not avoiding bad news, being open to suggestions and correcting a mistake that has been brought to his attention, this manager had not only earned the trust of this executive but also strengthened the place of values in challenging situations.

Values Dialogues

Sanjay: In my experience in the previous organization as well as here, being value oriented at the workplace is perceived as a sign of weakness. Value-oriented conduct is almost mocked at. With such a mindset being there, how do we instil values in the workplace?

Sheela: While there are people who voice this point of view, my own experience has convinced me that this view is absolutely baseless and in reality is very far from the truth.

Great thinkers across generations have said that values are actually a sign of strength and courage.

Sanjay: I too have read some of those quotes. But when I see people at the workplace talk this way, it instils an element of doubt. In fact, I remember an instance a close friend shared from her workplace. She was just a newcomer and a junior in this organization. She was asked to sign some vouchers by a senior member of the organization, for expenses which she had never incurred. She refused to do so. In response, all her boss said was, 'You are being naïve; nothing will happen. Don't worry'. She was quite surprised at this response from her boss. She of course refused to change her stance. But later on some of her senior colleagues even remarked that she was being stupid.

Sheela: Thanks for sharing that. Let us take that very instance. What made her stick to her stance? The important thing is that her own personal values clearly guided her to take that position, and without doubt she said she will not sign. Remember you said she was new to the organization and also was at a junior level. She could have been easily intimidated by the senior, and it could have been easy to agree to sign. But then how could she still hold on to her position?

Sanjay: Her courage?

Sheela: Indeed, and her conviction in what she stood for. Malcom X famously said, 'If you don't stand for something, you will fall for everything'. So clearly this is an act of strength, enabled by courage and conviction. Remember, there could be many things in your current set of circumstances that suggests and nudges you to take the other path, but it takes courage to win over those temptations.

Sanjay: What do you mean by temptations?

Sheela: Temptations could be numerous—pleasing the boss to stay in his/her good books, meeting one's targets, trying to cover up something, you want to appear nice in front of others, we don't want to share credit for the idea we have and so on. This is what Maya Angelou has to say:

> Courage is the most important of all the virtues, because without courage you can't practice any other virtue consistently.

Sanjay: What about kindness? Such softer virtues are seen as signs of weakness. Say one executive is known to be much kinder than the other, isn't he or she considered weaker too?

Sheela: See what has been said about that:

> Compassion and tolerance are not a sign of weakness, but a sign of strength.

—Dalai Lama

> Tenderness and kindness are not signs of weakness and despair, but manifestations of strength and resolution.

—Kahlil Gibran

Of course, we are assuming *ceteris paribus* condition of functional competence of compared executives. I am sure these quotations sufficiently answer your question.

Values Reflection

Introspect and deliberate upon these questions as you go forward in strengthening your organization's culture of values:

- List five values you like to see in others.
- List top five qualities that define you as an individual. How do they differ from the above?
- When it comes to upholding the values (that have been identified by your organization), what challenges do you face?
- As a manager, what are the obstacles your team faces in living the values identified by the organization? Draw up the list on your own, then gather feedback from the members of the team. How close was your assessment?

- What steps do you propose to take to strengthen your values (the core values of your organization)?
- One of your subordinates comes up to you and says: 'To me, being values oriented seems to be the natural state. But to some around me, compromising values seems to be a practical way of dealing with workplace situations. How do I deal with this dilemma?' How would you respond to the question?

**

धर्मो मातेव पुष्णाति धर्मः पाति पितेव च ।
धर्मः सखेव प्रीणाति धर्मः स्निह्यति बन्धुवत् ॥

Dharma nourishes like a mother; dharma protects like a father; dharma pleases like a friend; and dharma is affectionate like a relative.

—Subhaashitam

CONCLUSION

An Unshakeable Faith in Values

Everyone talks of value decline in the family, businesses, society, nation and the globe. And then we hear of the ancient Roman Civilization that collapsed because of erosion of values.

There are people who go to the extent of saying that 'business organizations are completely devoid of values'. Then there are those who say the same thing about family and society.

This is a serious matter and certainly calls for a closer introspection. This is primarily because each of us is a stakeholder in the society and also in the small unit which we call family.

A closer examination reveals that it would be incorrect to say that 'there are no values'. Any institution—family, business, society—is held in place because of values. Yes, you may say that it is not adequate or it needs to be strengthened.

In this book, we have addressed the subject of values in the context of business organizations. The subject of values being very fundamental, the principles remain the same, whether it is the family or the society or even the nation. These discussions are relevant even to other kinds of organizations, not only of the business kind—government, NGOs, public sector, etc.

Looking at the organization you belong to, you can examine the ideas discussed in this book, in the context of your immediate team, your department, business unit you belong to or the entire organization. The ideas remain the same because the individual who possesses or upholds the values is the same, whatever be the context.

The challenge before us is to instil the values in the institution we belong to. For that, what is the starting point? Yes, it is the individual! Let each one of us endeavour to examine his or her own position in the context of values. Once we address our own individual self, the rest will automatically follow.

Let's start with the important fact that values are there in place. Perhaps not all the values, but at least some values are there. Identify them. Make that the starting point.

You would have come across the idea of SWOT (strengths, weaknesses, opportunities and threats). Whenever we look at improvement, we recognize that we have strengths and weaknesses. It is difficult to imagine someone who says, 'No, I can't think of any strengths at all'. Similarly, let us recognize that values are there. Next step is what else do we need to move beyond where we are today and eventually get to where we want to be. Thus, you can prepare a game plan.

But, undoubtedly the starting point is belief.

Believe that values are critical.
Believe that family, business and society are grounded on values.
Believe that each of us has a responsibility, before we look at another.
Believe that this is our bequest to the next generation.
Believe that there are certain values that are already in place.
Believe that we can do it!
Believe that I can do it!

Let us also recognize and be prepared that there are opposing forces at play. There will be non-believers and sceptics. There are those who believe that the way businesses are structured, and in this dog-eat-dog world, the idea of having values in the business context is not a practical thing. Most people point to such views and opinions and become discouraged or cynical themselves.

Let us not forget that the cynicism people carry is based on their experiences across different roles, and organizations they have worked in. It is not just a feeling. They have been conditioned by the circumstances they faced. In fact, there is a popular saying which says, every cynical person is a disappointed idealist. There is only one solution—they have to see values in action to change their opinion. Also, good awareness mechanisms will go a long way in getting them on your side.

Once you have decided to get on to the inevitable journey of values, what is a good place to begin? Like anything else in the context of an organization, begin at the top. The question to ask is: Are the founders and/or the top management of the organization convinced that values are the most fundamental building block of a successful business organization? If they believe so, then you have a starting point.

Once this is established, then you have achieved the most important milestone in this values journey, that is, a convinced top management.

The bulk of the responsibility lies with the top team in the organization (the founders, the head of the organization and the rest of the senior management team). What are the next steps? Identify the values, live the values, provide a suitable atmosphere for values to thrive, be sensitive to how the organization's values culture is shaping up and bring in appropriate course correction, when required. The most crucial of these for the senior management is living the values, more popularly referred to as walking the talk.

The values that are very foundational for the senior management team to lead the organization and the employees in this journey of values are integrity, patience, humility and courage.

Many today say that technology is taking over everything, and in the times to come, machines driven by AI will replace the humans in many areas. Let us not forget that the very development of AI is in the hands of the humans. Also, as long as the human civilization lasts, the importance of values cannot be ignored because they are the most fundamental vocabulary of the human race.

Conclusion

In the case of organizations which feel that this values journey doesn't seem practical, here is another way of looking at it: If you are willing to spend time, effort and money on figuring out new strategies to enhance your business, then spending time on the most fundamental element of the organization—values—is not so unthinkable.

Let us make a sincere attempt to play our part in the context of the workplace. The starting part could be in the context of the small team we are a part of.

Remember, everyone is waiting for a nudge. A tiny move on your part, as an individual, could have a huge impact on the organization. The changes may not be visible immediately.

As an individual, there is only one golden rule, 'values are the very foundation of life', and it is our responsibility to uphold this rule. When we expect others to act in a certain manner which is agreeable to us, we owe it to them to be values oriented. This sentiment is summarized as the essence of dharma in the following verse:

श्रूयतां धर्मसर्वस्वं श्रुत्वा चाप्यवधार्यताम् ।
आत्मनः प्रतिकूलानि परेषां न समाचरेत् ॥

Listen to that in which is contained the entire dharma, and then instil them in your heart—'do not do unto others, that which is unfavourable to oneself'.

—Padma Puraanam

The second line of the verse captures the fundamental motivation to being values based.

Four-Part Test for Values-Oriented Decision-Making

When faced with a situation where you have to take a decision, as an individual, a team or an organization, apply the following simple guidelines:

- Is your decision in harmony with all other stakeholders in your ecosystem (including employees, customers, vendors, environment, employees, society)?
- Have your decision and its consequences (not just immediate but also long-term effects) been discussed with others in your team?
- Is your decision in alignment with the organization's values?
- Is your decision in alignment with the laws of the land?

In other words,

PAUSE—INTROSPECT—DISCUSS—DECIDE

Remember, these are just suggested guidelines and cannot be taken as the absolute set of rules for defining values-based thoughts or actions.

We close with an important point. There are different terms that are floating around: values, ethics, Codes of Conduct, principles and so on. Don't worry about the terms; just pick one that you are comfortable with. What matters is the intent behind it.

Let each one of us, as individuals, play a small part in this movement towards building a values-based business and society. Remember the famous adage: 'Rome was not built in a day!'

* * *

BIBLIOGRAPHY

Austin, Robert D. and Gary P. Pisano. 2017, May–June. 'Neurodiversity as a Competitive Advantage'. *Harvard Business Review*. 95 (3). Available at: https://hbr.org/2017/05/neurodiversity-as-a-competitive-advantage (accessed on 28 March 2019).

Catmull, Ed. 2014. *Creativity, Inc.: Overcoming the Unseen Forces That Stand in the Way of True Inspiration*. New York, NY: Random House.

Collins, Jim. 2001. *Good to Great*. New York, NY: Harper Collins.

Dalio, Ray. 2017. *Principles*. Westport, CT: Bridgewater Associates.

Garton, Eric and Michael Mankins. 2015, December. 'Engaging Your Employees Is Good, But Don't Stop There'. *Harvard Business Review*. Available at https://hbr.org/2015/12/engaging-your-employees-is-good-but-dont-stop-there (accessed on 24 December 2018).

Gentry, William A., Todd J. Weber and Golnaz Sadri. 'Empathy in the Workplace' (A White Paper). Centre for Creative Leadership. Available at https://www.ccl.org/wp-content/uploads/2015/04/EmpathyInTheWorkplace.pdf (accessed on 28 December 2018).

Haas, Martine and Mark Mortensen. 2016, June. 'The Secrets of Great Teamwork'. *Harvard Business Review*. Available at https://hbr.org/2016/06/the-secrets-of-great-teamwork (accessed on 24 December 2018).

Hill, Linda A., Greg Brandeau, Emily Truelove and Kent Lineback. 2014, June. 'Collective Genius'. *Harvard Business Review*. Available at https://hbr.org/2014/06/collective-genius (accessed on 28 March 2019).

Kaptein, Muel. 2012. 'Why Good People Sometimes Do Bad Things? 52 Reflections on Ethics at Work'. *Social Science*

Research Network. Available at: https://ssrn.com/abstract= 2117396 (accessed on 26 December 2018).

Lee, Su-Hyun and Tiffany May. 2018, July 28. 'Go Home, South Korea Tells Workers, as Stress Takes Its Toll'. *The New York Times*. Available at https://www.nytimes.com/2018/07/28/world/asia/south-korea-overwork-workweek.html (accessed on 27 March 2019).

Wallas, Graham. 2014 [1926]. *The Art of Thought*. Tunbridge Wells: Solis Press.

Waytz, Adam and Malia Mason. 2013, July–August. 'Your Brain at Work'. *Harvard Business Review*. Available at https://hbr.org/2013/07/your-brain-at-work (accessed on 28 March 2019).

Zenger, Jack and Joseph Folkman. 2014, 30 July. 'The Skills Leaders Need at Every Level'. *Harvard Business Review*. Available at https://hbr.org/2014/07/the-skills-leaders-need-at-every-level (accessed on 24 December 2018).

Online Resources

- The Corporate Scandal Sheet. http://www.forbes.com/2002/07/25/accountingtracker.html (accessed on 28 December 2018)
- Corporate Fraud in India Rose 45% Last Two Years: Study. http://articles.economictimes.indiatimes.com/2015–01-14/news/58066216_1_corporate-frauds-strong-internal-controls-tax-evasion (accessed on 28 December 2018)
- Business Ethics. https://en.wikipedia.org/wiki/Business_ethics (accessed on 28 December 2018)
- Business Ethics (Investopedia). http://www.investopedia.com/terms/b/business-ethics.asp#ixzz4ZQ4eSO7F (accessed on 28 December 2018)
- Code of Conduct for Members of Rajya Sabha. http://rajyasabha.nic.in/rsnew/members/code_conduct.pdf (accessed on 28 December 2018)
- LinkedIn's Jeff Weiner: How Compassion Builds Better Companies. http://knowledge.wharton.upenn.edu/article/linkedin-ceo-how-compassion-can-build-a-better-company/ (accessed on 28 December 2018)

- The Curious Case of Creativity. https://www,thinkwithgoogle. com/articles/the-curious-case-of-creativity.html (accessed on 28 December 2018)
- How to Kill Creativity, the Microsoft Way. http://www.inc. com/margaret-heffernan/how-to-kill-creativity.html (accessed on 28 December 2018)
- The Terrible Management Technique That Cost Microsoft Its Creativity. http://www.forbes.com/sites/frederickallen/ 2012/07/03/the-terrible-management-technique-that-cost-microsoft-its-creativity/ (accessed on 28 December 2018)
- 42.5% of Corporate Employees Suffer from Depression: ASSOCHAM. http://www.assocham.org/newsdetail.php?id= 4918 (accessed on 28 December 2018)
- 46% of Workforce in Firms in India Suffer from Some or the Other Form of Stress: Data. http://economictimes.indiatimes. com/jobs/46-of-workforce-in-firms-in-india-suffer-from-some-or-the-other-form-of-stress-data/articleshow/52696795. cms (accessed on 28 December 2018)
- Workplace Stress. https://stress.org/workplace-stress/ (accessed on 28 December 2018)
- Mental Health Crisis: 45 Million Working Days LOST Due to Stress, Anxiety and Depression. http://www.express.co.uk/ news/uk/661672/Mental-health-crisis-45-million-working-days-LOST-stress-anxiety-depression (accessed on 28 December 2018)
- 10 Health Problems Related to Stress That You Can Fix. http://www.webmd.com/balance/stress-management/features/ 10-fixable-stress-related-health-problems#1 (accessed on 28 December 2018)
- Workplace Suicides Are Rising and Globalization is to Blame. http://www.newsweek.com/workplace-suicides-are-rising-and-ceos-are-blame-490941 (accessed on 28 December 2018)
- 9 Things That Make Good Employees Quit. https://www. huffingtonpost.com/dr-travis-bradberry/9-things-that-make-good-e_b_8870074.html (accessed on 28 December 2018)
- Workers with Disabilities Solved This Company's Talent Crisis. https://hbr.org/2012/09/workers-with-disabilities-solv (accessed on 28 December 2018)

- The NCPEDP—Mindtree Helen Keller Awards. http://www.ncpedp.org/The_NCPEDP_Helen_Keller_Awards (accessed on 28 December 2018)
- How New Technology Helps Blind People Explore the World. https://www.ted.com/talks/chieko_asakawa_how_new_technology_helps_blind_people_explore_the_world (accessed on 28 December 2018)
- Disabilities and Inclusion: US Findings. http://www.talentinnovation.org/_private/assets/DisabilitiesInclusion_KeyFindings-CTI.pdf (accessed on 28 December 2018)
- The Case for Improving Work for People with Disabilities Goes Way Beyond Compliance. https://hbr.org/2017/12/the-case-for-improving-work-for-people-with-disabilities-goes-way-beyond-compliance (accessed on 28 December 2018)
- Why Companies Are Hiring People with Disabilities? https://economictimes.indiatimes.com/jobs/why-companies-are-hiring-people-with-disabilities/articleshow/61609438.cms (accessed on 28 December 2018)
- Business Mortality—Company Life Spans Reduced. http://cloudnames.com/en/blog/business-mortality/ (accessed on 28 December 2018)
- Guiding Principles at Toyota. https://www.toyota-global.com/company/vision_philosophy/guiding_principles.html (accessed on 28 December 2018)
- 6 Surprising Statistics about Stress Around the World. https://medium.com/@busy_lifestyle/6-surprising-statistics-about-stress-around-the-world-f60d5831c404 (accessed on 28 December 2018)
- Where Will We Find Tomorrow's Leaders. https://hbr.org/2008/01/where-will-we-find-tomorrows-leaders (accessed on 28 December 2018)
- Corporate Governance Badly Down at Infosys, Board Needs an Overhaul: NR Narayana Murthy. https://economictimes.indiatimes.com/articleshow/57070727.cms?utm_source = contentofinterest&utm_medium = text&utm_campaign = cppst (accessed on 28 December 2018)

- Humility Key to Effective Leadership. http://www.buffalo.edu/news/releases/2011/12/13065.html (accessed on 28 December 2018)
- The Founding Prospectus. https://www.sony.net/SonyInfo/CorporateInfo/History/prospectus.html (accessed on 28 December 2018)
- AirAsia's Chief Responds to Crisis with Quick Compassion. https://www.nytimes.com/2015/01/01/business/international/airasia-tony-fernandes-responds-to-crisis-with-quick-compassion.html (accessed on 28 December 2018)
- Top Ethics Official Resigns Says Working for Trump Requires 'Abandonment of Conscience'. https://www.commondreams.org/news/2017/07/03/top-ethics-official-resigns-says-working-trump-requires-abandonment-conscience (accessed on 28 December 2018)
- The Three Pillars of a Teaming Culture. https://hbr.org/2013/12/the-three-pillars-of-a-teaming-culture (accessed on 28 December 2018)
- Your Character When You're Alone. https://www.wnd.com/2011/03/273945/ (accessed on 28 December 2018)
- A Brief History of the 7-S ('McKinsey 7-S') Model. http://tompeters.com/2011/03/a-brief-history-of-the-7-s-mckinsey-7-s-model/ (accessed on 28 December 2018)
- IT Firms Manipulate Social Media for Poll Campaign. http://indianexpress.com/article/india/india-others/it-firms-manipulate-social-media-for-poll-campaign-cobrapost/ (accessed on 28 December 2018)
- List of Corporate Collapses and Scandals. http://en.wikipedia.org/wiki/List_of_corporate_collapses_and_scandals (accessed on 28 December 2018)
- The Enemy Within. http://www.economist.com/news/business/21597980-fraud-within-companies-risk-can-never-be-eliminated-just-managed-enemy-within?zid=317&ah=8a47fc455a44945580198768fad0fa41 (accessed on 28 December 2018)
- The 10 Worst Corporate Accounting Scandals of All Time. http://www.accounting-degree.org/scandals/ (accessed on 28 December 2018)

- 10 Biggest Corporate Frauds in the World. http://topyaps.com/top-10-frauds-of-corporate-world (accessed on 28 December 2018)
- Why Employees Commit Fraud. http://www.journalofaccountancy.com/Issues/2001/Feb/WhyEmployeesCommitFraud.htm (accessed on 28 December 2018)
- What is the Life Expectancy of Your Company? https://www.weforum.org/agenda/2015/01/what-is-the-life-expectancy-of-your-company/ (accessed on 28 December 2018)
- This is How Long Your Business Will Last, According to Science. http://time.com/3768559/company-mortality-rate-survival-study/ (accessed on 28 December 2018)
- Why Are So Many of the World's Oldest Businesses in Japan? https://priceonomics.com/why-are-so-many-of-the-worlds-oldest-businesses-in/ (accessed on 28 December 2018)
- How World's Oldest Family Businesses Have Survived for Centuries. https://www.businesstoday.in/opinion/columns/how-worlds-oldest-family-businesses-have-survived-for-centuries/story/264445.html (accessed on 28 December 2018)
- About Zappos Culture. https://www.zappos.com/core-values (accessed on 28 December 2018)
- Mumbai Dabbawala. http://mumbaidabbawala.in (accessed on 28 December 2018)
- Mission, Vision & Values. https://www.coca-colacompany.com/our-company/mission-vision-values (accessed on 28 December 2018)
- Dharma: Fundamental Code of Conduct. https://www.oberoigroup.com/careers/about_us/dharma.htm (accessed on 28 December 2018)
- Our Vision with Values. https://www.iocl.com/AboutUs/Vision.aspx (accessed on 28 December 2018)
- Culture & Values. https://www.cognizant.com/about-cognizant/cultural-values (accessed on 28 December 2018)
- Our Purpose, Values and Principles. https://www.pg.com/translations/pvp_pdf/english_PVP.pdf (accessed on 28 December 2018)

ABOUT THE AUTHORS

Br. Prasanna Swaroopa began his career in the IT industry serving it in various capacities, including software engineering, design, project management and general management. After having devoted 14 years to it, he exited the IT profession to explore and discover what lies beyond the usual avenues of employment. He then became a disciple of Swami Bhoomananda Tirtha and spent 12 years in Narayanashrama Tapovanam (an ashram in Kerala). This path of self-discovery enabled him to understand and realize the intricacies of the mind and their application to everyday life situations.

In the past, during his association with the Foundation for Restoration of National Values (FRNV), he was engaged in projects relating to reforms with the aim of creating a value-based society.

As a spiritual seeker, he is deeply engaged in the study of scriptures such as the Bhagavad Gita, the Upanishads and the works of the great philosopher–saint Adi Shankara. He devotes his time sharing his experience with others for exploring the path to well-being, excellence and creativity.

His workshops and writing emanate from the firm conviction that spiritual wisdom and values are a great source of strength to individuals in order to achieve happiness and personal fulfilment, and at the same time success in life. He is an alumnus of the Indian Institute of Technology, Delhi.

T. D. Chandrasekhar (called TD by friends) has been involved with businesses for three decades now, first as a practising executive and later as an external expert. In his current role as a coach, a facilitator and a consultant for over a decade, he has coached over 75 executives, and facilitated over 750 corporate programmes, covering more than 15,000 executives. As an invited speaker, he has addressed over 100 occasions, including initiatives such as TEDx. His focus has primarily been on excellence, creativity and innovation both at individual and organizational levels with leading business organizations in India and overseas.

His last corporate role was as Country Head, India, of Ameriprise Financial, which he set up and led till he started on his next phase. In his executive roles, he was known to focus both on professional excellence and personal well-being of staff as he believes strongly in the concept of sustainable business success.

He also loves interacting with students and is associated as a guest faculty at educational institutes such as IIT Delhi, IIM Lucknow, MDI Gurgaon, and Vedica Scholars, where he engages in discussion on topics related to creativity and factors facilitating growth of the mindset.

At home, his three-year-old twin daughters bring him unbounded joy.

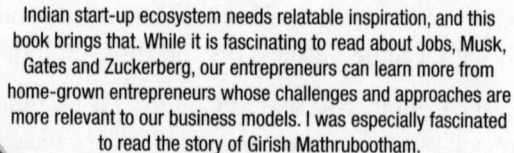

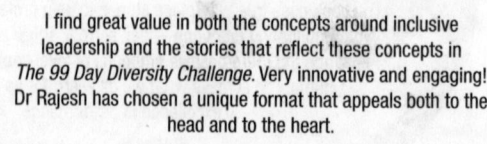